D1246340

# ADVOCATE FOR ANIMALS!

## AN ABOLITIONIST VEGAN HANDBOOK

Gary L. Francione
Anna Charlton

EXEMPLA PRESS

"Exempla" is the plural of "exemplum," or a story, which could be real or fictitious, used to make a moral point. Exemplary literature was a genre that was popular in classical, medieval, and Renaissance literature.

Read more about animal ethics in these other publications from Exempla Press:

*Animal Rights: The Abolitionist Approach* (2015)
www.abolitionistapproachbook.com

*Eat Like You Care: An Examination of the Morality of Eating Animals* (2013)
www.eatlikeyoucarebook.com

*For every Abolitionist who has been reluctant to speak out but who spoke out anyway.*

# Contents

# Acknowledgements

Thanks to all of the Abolitionist vegans whose excellent work is discussed in these pages. And thanks to Cristina Cubells and Frances McCormack, who read the manuscript and made very helpful editorial suggestions, and to Cristina, who designed and formatted the book.

# A Thought Before We Begin

Abolitionists maintain that the animal rights movement is a social justice movement that seeks to end animal exploitation and not to make that exploitation more "humane." In order to end animal exploitation as a social matter, we must convince people to end exploitation in their own lives.

We must convince them to go vegan.

Each person who does vegan education is on the front line of the effort to give a voice to the interests of animals who are otherwise ignored. We have the moral obligation to speak out about veganism to every person we can in every situation we can. We have an obligation to do the very best job that we can educating people about veganism. We are in the only social justice movement where our constituents cannot tell us we are performing badly and fire us if we let them down.

The purpose of this book is to help you to become an effective Abolitionist vegan advocate.

# Introduction

## Abolitionist Veganism

### The Problem

Since the beginning of time, there have been—in total—about 110 billion humans who have lived and died.

We kill *more* nonhuman animals than that *every single year*.

Think about that for a second. Our exploitation of nonhumans represents violence on a scale that is unparalleled.

The largest number of animals we kill is for food—about 60 billion land animals and at least one trillion sea animals killed annually. And there are many billions more killed every year for various other reasons, including biomedical research, entertainment, and sport.

One thing is crystal clear and undisputable: this horrible and pervasive animal exploitation is not going to end anytime soon.

So the question is: if we care about the exploitation of animals—if we think that animals matter morally—what should we do *now?*

## The Solution: Abolition

If we believe that animals matter morally, there is one and only one answer: we must seek to abolish animal exploitation. It's not a matter of making exploitation more "humane." It's a matter of *abolishing* exploitation.

What does abolition involve?

Abolition involves embracing an *animal rights* position and maintaining that, just as we reject the chattel slavery of humans, we must reject the status of nonhuman animals as our *property*. Only then can they be recognized as nonhuman persons.

Abolition involves a clear and explicit rejection of the *animal welfare* position—the idea that it is morally acceptable to use animals as long as we treat them in a "humane" way.

And in order to abolish animal exploitation as a social matter, we must abolish animal exploitation from our individual lives.

That means that *we*—those of us who agree that we should abolish animal exploitation—must go vegan. We must stop eating, wearing, or using animals and animal products to the extent practicable.

And we must engage in creative, nonviolent vegan advocacy in order to convince others to go vegan.

Abolitionists see the animal rights movement as a *social justice* movement and view being vegan as a matter of our being just. *Veganism is about justice.* If animals matter morally—if they are nonhuman persons—then we have a moral obligation to reject their institutional-ized exploitation and to not eat, wear, or use them.

For Abolitionists, veganism is a *moral imperative*. This means that it is something we have a *moral obligation* to do. It is not an option any more than is our not participating in the violation of fundamental human rights. Abolitionists see veganism as a rejection of and resistance to the victimization of the vulnerable that is considered as "normal" in our speciesist society. They reject violence and see veganism as a necessary component of a nonviolent life.

Abolitionist veganism reflects a profound revolution within the individual; a complete rejection of the paradigm of oppression and violence that they have been taught from childhood to accept as the natural order. It changes their life and the lives of those with whom they share this vision of nonviolence. Abolitionist veganism is anything but passive; on the contrary, it is the active refusal to cooperate with injustice.

For Abolitionist vegans, veganism is not a matter of "compassion" or "mercy." It is an obligation of justice that requires that we respect the fundamental rights of nonhumans just as justice requires that we respect the fundamental rights of humans.

## But Can Vegan Advocacy Work?

It certainly can. In fact, it's the *only* thing that can work. We aren't going to get people to stop exploiting animals by making animal exploitation supposedly more "humane." That will just make people more comfortable about continuing to exploit animals.

And because animals are property, it costs money to protect animal interests, and the standards of animal treatment will always be very low anyway. The very concept of "humane" exploitation is nothing more than a fantasy, and one that is designed to encourage people to perpetuate their animal exploitation.

We are not going to end animal exploitation by making people think that eating dog meat or killing marine mammals is worse than eating cows or chickens or killing any other sentient being. We won't get anywhere promoting the idea that wearing fur is worse than wearing leather or wool, or that wearing fur is worse than eating animals.

There is only one way that we can end animal exploitation: convincing other people that exploiting animals is wrong and persuading them to stop participating in it.

If we do the math, we see that this is not only possible—it's very efficient.

Let's assume that there are one million vegans in the United States. That is a ridiculously low estimate but that is precisely why we are using it —it's not controversial. The United States has a population of approximately 325 million people. If every one of those one million

7

vegans persuaded *one* other person in the next year to go vegan, there would be two million. If, in the following year, every one of those two million vegans persuaded one other person to go vegan, we'd have four million. And then eight million, and then 16 million, 32 million, 64 million, 128 million, 256 million and, in year 10, the entire population would be vegan even if the number of people rose (and let's hope it doesn't) to 512 million.

Let's assume that there are 500,000 vegans in the United Kingdom. Again, that's a low estimate. The UK has a population of 65 million. So repeat the calculation with every vegan persuading just one person to go vegan in the next year, and there will be a vegan UK in seven years.

People who, for moral reasons, do not eat, wear, or use animals and animal products don't go to zoos, Sea World, rodeos, or bullfights. They don't ride around in carriages pulled by horses. So a decision to go vegan not only results in a decrease in the demand for animals to be killed for food, but decreases the demand to exploit animals in all other contexts.

## What Do We Mean by "Creative" Vegan Advocacy?

Animal exploitation is "normal." Most people eat, wear, and use animals. They don't see this as morally objectionable. This is not to say that they don't care about animals. They do. Many care a great deal. They want animals to be "humanely" treated—whatever that means. But they have never questioned animal *use* as a general matter. Some have assumed that if we don't eat animal products, we will be unhealthy. Some have assumed that it's just "natural" to use animals without ever really thinking about what that means. Some had other reasons that have led them to not question animal use and to consider that they should reject all animal use in their own lives.

The goal of "creative" vegan advocacy is to get people to see that, if animals matter morally, they are committed to stop using animals as resources and to go vegan.

The goal is getting people to see that the solution to the problem of animal exploitation is not for them to write a check to one of the many large animal welfare charities that seek larger cages for animals or that target the consumption of dog meat in China.

The goal is getting them to see that the problem is not something they give money to someone *else* to address; it's a problem that *they* address by going vegan in the first instance, and then convincing others to go vegan.

Creative vegan advocacy is *any* advocacy that gets people to think about the problem of animal exploitation in a different way—as one of *use* and not merely of *treatment*, and that gets them to consider abolishing animal exploitation in their own lives and helping others to do the same. Sure, it is better to impose less suffering on animals than more. But even if we (supposedly) make the treatment more "humane," the exploitation would still be morally wrong. "Humane" slavery is still slavery.

Creative vegan advocacy can take many forms, and we explore some of those in this book. The common denominator is the message. Abolitionists maintain that, if animals matter morally, we need to stop treating them as things that have no moral value. We must start thinking of animals as *nonhuman persons*—as beings who matter morally. And that excludes using them for food, clothing, etc.

Abolitionists talk about veganism. They don't talk about being "veg" or "veggie." They don't use words like "veg*n." They talk about veganism as a moral obligation. They don't characterize veganism as any sort of sacrifice but as a joy in that vegans no longer participate in the victimization of the vulnerable.

Abolitionists don't see veganism as a concept to be avoided; they see it as *the* central concept of the animal rights movement. They see it as the most important single act of activism on behalf of animals they can take.

Although some people may adopt a vegan diet for health reasons, or out of concern for the environment, an Abolitionist vegan sees veganism first and foremost as a matter of moral obligation. An Abolitionist vegan may have health or environmental concerns as well, but the primary motivating force for the Abolitionist vegan is morality.

## What Do We Mean by "Nonviolent" Vegan Advocacy?

Abolitionists embrace nonviolence. They see veganism as an important component of a nonviolent life. Abolitionists maintain that our vegan advocacy ought itself to be nonviolent. Abolitionists never engage in physical violence against others.

As we will explain in this book, a central tenet of Abolitionist advocacy is that we should not judge individuals; we should focus on actions and practices. That is, Abolitionists do not condemn nonvegans; they seek to educate them so that they see that exploiting animals is something that is not consistent with thinking about animals as having moral value.

Moreover, because Abolitionists see the inextricable relationship between human rights and animal rights, they reject all forms of human discrimination both as a social matter and in their vegan advocacy.

## Why "Abolitionist"?

Why are we using "Abolitionist" with a capital A, rather than just using "abolitionist"?

The reason is that we are referring to a particular way of thinking about abolition—*the Abolitionist Approach to Animal Rights*, which we have developed over the past 30 or so years. We have discussed this theory in a number of places and publications, most recently, in our book, *Animal Rights: The Abolitionist Approach*.

There are Six Principles that comprise the Abolitionist Approach to Animal Rights. These Six Principles are contained, along with a brief summary, in Appendix 1.

This book will focus primarily on Principle Three, which provides: *Abolitionists maintain that veganism is a moral baseline and that creative, nonviolent vegan education must be the cornerstone of rational animal rights advocacy.*

In discussing Principle Three, we will also bring in consideration of Principle One, which provides: *Abolitionists maintain that all sentient beings, human or nonhuman, have one right—the basic right not to be treated as the property of others;* and Principle Two, which provides: *Abolitionists maintain that our recognition of this one basic right means that we must abolish, and not merely regulate, institutionalized animal exploitation, and that Abolitionists should not support welfare reform campaigns or single-issue campaigns.* In Chapter 12, we will consider briefly some advocacy suggestions concerning the other Principles.

We assume that most of the people who are reading this book have already read *Animal Rights: The Abolitionist Approach* and they are in agreement with the theory but want practical guidance on how to engage in creative, nonviolent vegan advocacy. If you have not yet read that book, you should consider doing so because it will help you to understand the Six Principles of the Abolitionist Approach.

There are some who think that theory is a waste of time because they want to be "activists." That position is transparently wrong. Theory *is absolutely* necessary; without theory we cannot know what action to choose to take. In the absence of a consideration of theory, the action chosen will be that prescribed by the agenda set by the status quo. In the animal context, the status quo is dominated by corporate welfarist charities. And that is why most "animal advocates" do nothing more than serve as unpaid labor for these reactionary groups that promote the concept of "humane" exploitation, or tell people that eating dogs is morally different from eating chickens, and that they can continue to eat chickens as long as they give donations to fund campaigns focused on eating dogs.

If you want to educate others to help animals, you must first educate yourself so that you understand the thinking behind veganism as a moral imperative. Our earlier book will provide you with a full understanding of the Six Principles of the Abolitionist Approach.

There are some animal advocates who refer to themselves as "abolitionist" but who don't subscribe to one or more of the Six Principles. For example, many animal advocates claim that they want to abolish animal exploitation in the long run but they do not advocate veganism as a moral imperative and, instead, promote campaigns for more "humane" exploitation or campaigns to reduce the consumption of meat, dairy, and other animal products. Those who promote "humane" exploitation or reduced consumption cannot be "abolitionist" as we use that term. We reject those positions just as we would reject promoting "humane" rape as a supposed means to the end of ending rape, or promoting war as a supposed means to having peace. A person who promotes "humane" slavery as a supposed means to the end of abolishing slavery is using "abolition" in a different way from the way in which someone who rejects all slavery is using it.

Abolitionists believe that the means that we choose to achieve abolition must be consistent with the end. Promoting exploitation and rights violation is not consistent with claiming to be an abolitionist with respect to that exploitation and those rights violations. The only means to the end of abolition that is consistent with that end is being crystal clear that all animal exploitation is morally wrong and that means recognizing that our personal participation in that exploitation is morally wrong. That means that we recognize veganism as a moral obligation.

## What Is Meant by "To the Extent Practicable"?

We maintain that a vegan is someone who does not eat, wear, or use animals or animal products to the extent practicable. What is meant by the expression "to the extent practicable"? Does it mean that we should be vegans but that it is acceptable to exploit animals when we find it convenient to do so? No, of course not. If it were, then being a "flexible vegan," or someone who is sometimes a vegan and sometimes eats, wears, or uses animal products, would be fine—and it isn't.

So what, exactly, do we mean by the use of "practicable"?

Basically, something is not "practicable" if we have no real choice to not do it.

For example, billions of animals are exploited by humans, and animal by-products are in plastics, road surfaces, etc. So it is simply not possible to avoid all animal products just as we cannot avoid driving on roads that were originally laid by slaves. But where we have the ability to choose—and, unless we are stranded on a desert island, adrift at sea, or in some other unusual situation, we have choices concerning what we will eat, wear, and use—we have an obligation to not participate in exploiting animals just as we have an obligation not to violate the fundamental rights of other humans.

It is important to understand that saying that we have an obligation not to participate in animal exploitation to the extent practicable does not mean that we can eat, wear, or use animals whenever it's inconvenient not to do so. For example, we frequently get questions like, "what do you do when you are in an airport and can't get anything vegan to eat?" We don't know because we have *never* been in an airport ever where we could not find a banana or apple even if we could not get anything else. When someone tells us that they consumed animal products in an airport because a banana or apple or package of nuts was insufficient, and they wanted something more substantial, we explain that minor inconvenience does not mean ignoring important moral principles. "Not practicable" does not mean "not convenient." It is closer in meaning to "not possible."

What about eating food that has small amounts of animal by-products, such a candy bar that contains casein or whey, or potatoes that have been cooked in oil in which meat has been cooked? Eating animal products is not acceptable just because it's a relatively small quantity of animal products involved. Unless you are on a desert island starving to death and you have nothing to eat except a candy bar with animal ingredients or potatoes cooked in oil that has animal fat in it, it's completely practicable to avoid such products by choosing to eat a piece of fruit or waiting until you get home to eat.

Will the growing and harvesting of crops involve harm to animals? Yes. When we engage in any action—whether it involves producing plant foods or anything else—we will cause incidental and unintended harm to nonhumans and to humans. For example, humans are accidentally injured and killed in the production of every product we consume. But we distinguished this incidental and unintended harm and death to humans from deliberately murdering humans. Similarly, Abolitionists maintain that we should exercise care in all of our activities but they recognize that there will be inevitable unintended and incidental harm to animals. Abolitionists reject all *deliberate* harm and all *direct* participation in animal exploitation. Abolitionists reject all *institutional* animal exploitation. That is, they object to the use of animals as economic commodities and their resulting status as commodities or resources for human consumption.

## A Note About Our Focus

Veganism means not eating, wearing, or using animals to the extent practicable. So veganism is not just about what we eat. But many of the examples we give here will involve food.

The reason for this focus is that, in our 35 years of experience both as vegans and as animal rights advocates, nothing changes until the light goes on and people see that the primary way in which they interact with nonhuman animals—*as food*—is problematic. That is, as long as people are eating animals and animal products, their most significant form of animal exploitation remains part of their lives and they almost always participate in other forms of exploitation. Once they see that they can no longer justify treating nonhuman animals as food, everything changes. Someone who stops eating animals because they understand veganism as a moral imperative involving fundamental justice does not go out and buy leather shoes or go to a circus that uses animals.

## It's About YOU!

The Abolitionist position is, for the most part, promoted by *grassroots* advocates. That is, these advocates are not employed by, or supported by, and do not support, the large corporate animal charities. Moreover, most Abolitionists do not seek donations from the public. They choose advocacy methods that require little cost and fund their own advocacy activities, or, if they seek financial assistance, they do so only from other Abolitionists. But whatever they do, they *never* change or adapt their message in order to get donations.

If the paradigm is ever going to shift, it will be because there is a grassroots movement that is promoting a simple, clear, and unequivocal message: if animals matter morally at all, we cannot eat them, wear them, or otherwise use them as human resources. At the center of that message is a simple idea: go vegan and stop participating in the victimization of vulnerable nonhumans.

*But a grassroots movement means* **you.**

It means that this is not something we can delegate to others. This is something that each of us who cares has a responsibility to make happen. We may all contribute in different ways. Indeed, this book is about the different ways that we can contribute. But we must *all* contribute. This is our *collective* obligation.

*Never underestimate the power of one person:* **you.**

*You* have the ability to play a significant role in this grassroots abolitionist movement. Indeed, the *only* way that this can work is if you and others who are like-minded help others to see that veganism is the only rational response to the recognition that animals are not property. We reiterate what we said above: if everyone who is now vegan convinces one other person in the next year to go vegan, and this pattern repeats itself, the world would actually be vegan in a fairly short period of time. Unfortunately, that isn't going to happen, but it gives you a sense of the power of the individual.

You *can* make a difference.

You *must* make a difference.

## Changing the Conversation

At the present time, the social discussion about animals is focused on *treatment* and how to "improve" animal exploitation. That is, most people embrace the *animal welfare* position and assume that it's morally acceptable to use animals as long as we treat them "humanely." Abolitionists, who promote an *animal rights* approach, are seeking to get people to think about animal *use* and question whether we can justify using animals at all, rather than asking whether our treatment of the animals we exploit is "humane."

According to social scientists, if we had 10% of the population firmly convinced that no animal use can be justified, that would result in the spread of that idea and we would be having a different social discussion. See https://goo.gl/dErsNQ. We'd be talking about animal rights rather than talking about animal welfare. We'd be talking about whether veganism is the position we are obligated to adopt if we regard animals as having moral value rather than talking about how to be more "compassionate" animal exploiters.

And the change would begin to be apparent quickly. All we need to do is to convince 10% of the population—a small portion of the people out there who really do care about animals—to effect the spread of that idea and we would be having a different social discussion. The paradigm would begin to shift.

So let's change the conversation. Again, the individual—*you*—can play a role in getting us to that 10% so that we can do exactly that.

We want to help you become the excellent Abolitionist vegan advocate we know you can be. That is what this book is designed to help you to do.

## Outline of the Book

The book is divided into two parts:

**Part One** concerns the "how" of advocacy.

In Chapter 1, we examine ten guidelines that should inform your activism.

In Chapter 2, we discuss where to advocate.

In Chapter 3, we provide some reflections and ideas from those engaged in grassroots vegan advocacy.

In Chapter 4, we discuss vegan advocacy in situations of economic challenge.

**Part Two** concerns the "what" of advocacy—the substance of your advocacy.

In Chapter 5, we talk about getting people to see that there is no difference between the animals whom they love or care about and those whom they eat or wear.

In Chapter 6, we discuss veganism and the concept of "unnecessary suffering."

In Chapter 7, we focus on veganism and the concept of rights.

In Chapter 8, we discuss how to deal with other animal advocates who reject veganism as a moral baseline.

In Chapter 9, we present some brief notes on dealing with family and friends.

In Chapter 10, we consider how to deal with those who want to go vegan but are anxious about doing so.

In Chapter 11, we discuss how to deal with objections to veganism that you encounter during your advocacy.

In Chapter 12, we consider some ideas about advocating other aspects of the Abolitionist Approach.

In Appendix 1, after the brief Conclusion, we include all of the Six Principles of the Abolitionist Approach and a short summary of each.

In Appendix 2, we describe ten logical fallacies so that you are better equipped to make logical arguments.

Please note: we often use the singular "they" when we are referring to humans to reflect current discussions about sex and gender.

# Part One: The *How* of Abolitionist Vegan Advocacy

In this portion of the book, we will talk about some of the "nuts and bolts" of advocacy:

In Chapter 1, we will discuss ten general principles that, we hope, will help you to frame your advocacy.

In Chapter 2, we will discuss where you should advocate. Here's a preview: anywhere and everywhere!

In Chapter 3, a number of Abolitionist vegan advocates will share their thoughts with us about the various sorts of advocacy they do.

In Chapter 4, we will explore the challenge of Abolitionist vegan advocacy in situations of economic deprivation.

# Chapter 1

## Ten Simple Guidelines of Abolitionist Vegan Advocacy

In this chapter, we want to focus on some practical aspects of getting started as an Abolitionist vegan advocate.

So often, when we speak about animal advocacy, people have said to us, "that's great, but I could never do that." Our response is simple: "Yes, you can, and yes, you must!" We offer the following ten simple guidelines that we urge you to incorporate into *all* of your advocacy, irrespective of whether you are doing one-on-one discussion with a friend or a family member, talking with people who come up to your table, lecturing to a class, speaking to a packed auditorium, or having online discussions.

### Guideline #1: Advocate in role.

Many people are not natural public speakers. Indeed, speaking in public is the number one social fear! Added to the anxiety that many people feel about public speaking is the fact that, when people who care about animals are speaking about animal rights and veganism even to small groups of family and friends, they become emotionally invested and this hinders their communication.

Here is our suggestion: When you are advocating, remove yourself from the situation. *It's not about you*. It's about the animals who have no voice and on whose behalf you are speaking. Go into the role of being an advocate for the animals as you would if you were a lawyer advocating for a client. Many people do not know that some of the most successful trial lawyers are, on a personal level, shy people. They can represent others when they are in the role of advocate because, at that moment, they are advocating for someone else. They are speaking in role on behalf of their client.

Being a successful advocate for justice for animals—or, indeed, being a successful advocate for justice in any context—requires that you make a decision not to "psychologize" yourself out of your moral responsibility. You see advocating for animals as your job—as something you *must* do irrespective of your comfort level. You recognize that this is not about *you*. This is about *them*. You think of yourself as a lawyer who has been retained by a client who needs your help. You don't have the option not to advocate; you *must* advocate. It's your responsibility to advocate. Your "client's" life hangs in the balance.

Does this require some focus and determination? Yes, it does. But if you are going to help to address the pervasive violence and injustice—the victimization of the vulnerable that is animal exploitation—you do not have a choice. We must all be determined to stretch ourselves beyond our comfort level. We must stretch beyond shyness. We must stretch beyond fear. We must stretch beyond embarrassment.

Our disposition or our personal feelings may cause us to choose one means of communication, one type of advocacy, over another, and we can all discover where our strengths lie and where we are most effective. But the bottom line is that we cannot excuse ourselves from acting. You may be nervous, self-conscious, embarrassed, or shy when you first start and as you work toward being a more effective advocate. But you cannot hide behind those feelings and proffer them as an excuse for not acting on your deeply held moral convictions—the ones that define who you are. We live at a time when, it seems, that it is our *feelings* that determine what we will do. But our feelings are irrelevant to the situation in which animals find themselves. There is no balancing of our feelings and their predicament.

Think about it this way: If you agree that really missing cheese is not an excuse for not going vegan, why is being shy or nervous about speaking a good reason not to speak out for the animals? If you wouldn't accept the "I would be so sad if I couldn't eat cheese" excuse that we all hear all the time from others, why accept the "I am shy and nervous" excuse from yourself?

Find your authentic voice and then speak out, if not with confidence at first, then with determination.

## Guideline #2: Assume that people are good at heart.

Our default position when we talk with people ought to be that they are good at heart, and interested in, and educable about, moral issues. *They want to do the right thing.* There is a tendency among at least some advocates to have a very misanthropic view of other humans and to see them as being inherently immoral or uninterested in issues of morality. We disagree with that view.

If someone really is uninterested in moral issues, they probably won't talk with you in the first place. So if they are talking with you, assume that they are interested, they want to learn, and they are interested in doing the right thing.

Educate them. The animals are depending on *you* to do so.

## Guideline #3: Be patient: Appreciate that you may be speaking with someone who has never considered the issue before.

Animal exploitation involves a violation of fundamental rights. In this sense, it is analogous to the violation of the fundamental rights of humans. The problem is that, for most people, this analogy is anything but clear. This is not, however, because, as some "animal advocates" claim, animal exploitation is "invisible."

There is nothing "invisible" about animal exploitation. On the contrary, animal exploitation is *very* visible.

The problem is that most people have bought into the welfarist idea that animal exploitation is completely normal; that it is not a violation of the rights of animals; that it is an affirmation of the rights of humans to use animals as long as animals are treated in a supposedly "humane" way. Most people think that it's perfectly fine for *us* to use *them*. They may have concerns about animals not being treated "humanely," but they do not object per se to animal use. Indeed, they've never even questioned whether use itself is morally permissible.

If you are speaking with someone who, up to this point in their lives, has never considered this issue before, you cannot expect them to understand the analogy between human rights and nonhuman rights violations, and the consequent gravity of the latter, right from the start. You need to be mindful of this as you educate people. You don't teach math to children by starting with calculus.

We believe that patience is *the* most important characteristic that a good educator can have. Most people will not learn if the teacher is impatient; most people will learn if the teacher is patient. Being patient does *not* mean that you compromise in any way the message that animal use—however supposedly "humane"—is unjust; it just means that you are patient when you teach that uncompromised message.

Always be patient. You will get asked the same question many times; you will be asked questions that indicate you must start at the beginning with someone. But if you want to be an effective educator, you have to answer every question as if it were the first time you heard it. If you want others to be enthusiastic about your message, *you* have to be enthusiastic about it first. If you have to explain things again—or many times over—do it in a cheerful way.

## Guideline #4: Speak *with* others and not *at* or *to* them.

View those you speak with as "pre-vegan." We say, "speak with" not "speak at" or "speak to" because you will engage with someone more productively if you understand and respect their position and their experience. They are where most of us were once.

Treat them as having the moral impulse to understand your message and the moral framework to integrate that message into their ethical outlook. This does *not* mean that you should not be clear that all animal exploitation is morally wrong and veganism is morally required. You must be clear about those matters. But it does mean that when we talk with someone, you speak with empathy in your heart. That can only help the educational process.

## Guideline #5: Always be clear that you are judging actions and not individuals.

In the 5th century, St. Augustine wrote the phrase "Cum dilectione hominum et odio vitiorum," which means "With love for mankind and hatred of sins." This became popularized by Gandhi as "Hate the sin, love the sinner."

This is good advice. We should not judge another person because we can't really see into her or his heart. But we can judge conduct as right or wrong. And when conduct involves imposing suffering and death on others, we not only should judge that conduct, we *must* judge it. That is what it means to take morality seriously.

Applying this to the animal context, we can say, for example, that we are not going to judge those who engage in animal exploitation but we are going to be clear that animal exploitation is morally wrong. Although we must be clear that animal exploitation is unjust, we must also recognize that we are living at a time when people are inclined to take any criticism of what they are doing as a criticism of *them*. So when you say, for example, "using animals for food is morally wrong," many people who eat animals may hear, "I am judging you to be a bad person."

So when we discuss veganism with someone who is not a vegan, we should always be careful to point out that we are not judging them. We are judging *actions*. We are judging the institutionalized exploitation of nonhuman animals. And we judge it to be wrong. We must always remember that we have a moral obligation that we owe to the animals never to apologize for the message that all animal use is morally unjustifiable.

## Guideline #6: Use analogies carefully.

Analogies—comparisons between things—are useful if they help to elucidate a discussion. But the poorly explained or heavy-handed use of analogy can be counterproductive. In connection with not making value judgments about people, make sure that when you use analogies that involve the violation of the fundamental rights of humans, you are careful to explain that when you use those analogies you are not accusing nonvegans of violating those fundamental human rights. Rushing to use such analogies in a brief discussion often results in nothing useful; it teaches nothing and it may alienate your listener.

For example, murder, rape, and pedophilia involve fundamental rights violations. They involve treating human persons as though they were nothing but things. Engaging in animal exploitation similarly involves fundamental rights violations and involves treating nonhuman persons as things.

But there is a difference. It is not a *moral* difference, but a *psychological* one. Nevertheless, that psychological difference matters. Therefore, if you compare using and killing animals to rape, murder, pedophilia, etc., always make clear that you are *not* accusing those who are not vegans of being murders, rapists, child molesters, etc.

Let's take your dear grandparents who have been making Thanksgiving dinner for your family for many years. The centerpiece of that dinner is a dead bird and many of the things on the table contain eggs, dairy, etc.

Does that Thanksgiving dinner involve fundamental rights violations? Yes, absolutely. Are your grandparents and any members of your family who consume those foods treating nonhuman animals as nothing but things that lack moral value? Yes, absolutely.

Is that Thanksgiving dinner analogous to other fundamental rights violations, such as murder, rape, or pedophilia? Yes, absolutely. All of these actions involve treating human persons as things.

So does that mean that your grandparents are no different from Jack the Ripper?

No, that's not what it means.

Moral culpability is in large part a matter of *intention*. When someone engages in murder, rape, or pedophilia, they are intending to engage in actions that they recognize violate the fundamental rights of their victims. They may have all sorts of reasons why they think it's acceptable to do what they are doing in the particular situation. But they are intending to do an action that they *know* violates the fundamental rights of others.

Most people don't recognize that animal use per se involves rights violations. That's the problem. People are very confused about animal ethics. Most people think that although animals matter morally, it is alright to use and kill them as long as we provide an acceptable level of treatment. People are confused about whether we need to eat animals for health purposes. People are confused by the so-called "experts"—the large animal welfare charities that promote the "humane" exploitation of animals, reducetarianism, etc.

Most people have never even considered animal use to involve a matter of justice. Most people have never been confronted with the argument that animal use is morally wrong irrespective of how we treat animals.

Our job is to educate people. Our job is to get them to see that *all* fundamental rights violations are wrong and that just as murder, rape, and pedophilia involve violating the fundamental rights of humans, so eating, wearing, and otherwise using nonhuman animals violates their fundamental rights.

But if you call someone a murderer or rapist—or anything else horrible like that—you have said, in essence, they are an immoral person who is deliberately violating the rights of others.

If you do that, you lose them.

## Guideline #7: Always be clear that animal exploitation is wrong and that veganism is the moral baseline.

Many so-called "animal advocates" take the position that we cannot maintain that animal exploitation is morally wrong and that veganism is the moral baseline because many people disagree and we cannot tell people what to do. But that is like saying that we cannot say racism is morally wrong because there are people who are racists and we cannot tell them that racism is wrong.

If ours is a movement for justice for nonhuman animals, we can *never* be reluctant to condemn injustice. The "animal movement" is the *only* movement in human history where so-called advocates have been unwilling to do so.

We must clear in our message that we cannot justify animal use—however "humane" it may be. We must be clear that if animals matter morally, we cannot justify eating, wearing, or otherwise using animals. Any animal use violates the fundamental rights of animals not to be used as things or resources.

When "animal advocates" say that we cannot expect the world to go vegan overnight and, therefore, vegans must promote "baby steps," we must always be clear: *veganism is the moral baseline; veganism is required.* If someone cares about animals but is not willing to go vegan immediately, they can choose whatever interim steps they want to choose. But animal rights advocates should never be in a position of advocating for or approving those interim steps.

Some "animal advocates" claim that it's wrong to say that the *conduct* of animal exploitation is morally wrong. That is, they say that we should not only not judge the person who is, for example, consuming cage-free eggs, but also that we should not reject "cage-free" eggs as involving animal exploitation because that would not be "compassionate" toward the person who is consuming the "happy" eggs as it would "shame" them. They turn the principle "Hate the sin, love the sinner" into "We must love the sin in order to love the sinner." That position is absurd and clearly promotes animal exploitation. Abolitionists reject it categorically.

## Guideline #8: Do not assume that people are stupid.

Many animal advocates believe that the general public is not able to understand the arguments in favor of veganism and that, because of this supposed inability, we must not promote veganism directly. They claim that instead of talking about veganism, we should talk about vegetarianism, Meatless Monday, "happy" meat and other animal products, and just about anything except veganism.

We disagree. People are not stupid. Some may not be highly educated in a formal sense but that does not mean that they are not able to understand why veganism is a moral baseline. We have heard animal advocates say things like we need to be mindful of "the limitations of ordinary people," who supposedly do not possess the requisite "intellectual and moral abilities" needed to understand veganism as a moral imperative, or that some people just can't understand moral principles. That's elitist nonsense. We believe—based on doing this work for 35 years—that *anyone* and *everyone* can understand the ideas that inform Abolitionist veganism.

We think that people ought always to be clear in their educational efforts and not use jargon or unnecessary complexity irrespective of who they are talking with. Advocacy efforts are not the same thing as academic presentations. If someone with whom we are speaking wants to discuss the matter of animal ethics in more philosophical, jurisprudential, or theoretical ways, we are pleased to do so. But, for the most part, keeping ideas simple is the best way to go. There is no mystery here; there is nothing complicated. People can understand if we teach effectively. If people don't understand, it's generally because we have not been good teachers!

## Guideline #9: Do not get defensive. Respond, don't react.

Yes, some people will try to provoke us or will ask questions or make comments that we will find insulting or that we will take as not being serious. For example, there is *no one* who has been vegan for longer than five minutes who has not had someone ask: "What about plants? You're killing them when you eat salad" or something similarly absurd. Far from getting upset when someone asks such a question, we regard it as a sign that the person really has very little else to say and does not know how to engage the issue. The person may feel uncomfortable so they ask a silly question. It is precisely that sort of person who can be educated but it is important that you don't allow the silly question to result in your ending the conversation.

We are not denying that there are people who are not serious and don't want to have serious discussion, so they ask a silly question because they wrongly think it's humorous and they are not aware you've heard it many times before. But if they are interested in the issue and they ask such a question, you may be closer to being able to educate them than you think.

Sometimes, people will make a rude or sarcastic comment. If the comment is really offensive, you may decide to end the conversation. But often, such comments are an indication that the topic makes the person uncomfortable and they deal with that discomfort in an awkward or inappropriate way. In such situations (and assuming you are not offended and have decided to end the conversation), you need to make a judgment about whether the person is really interested in a serious discussion, if so, overlook the comment and start a serious discussion. You will know almost immediately whether you've called it right.

A general rule that we use is that if someone is really not interested in what we are saying, they will, as a general matter, walk away. Treat every comment and question—even the ones you find abrasive, rude, or sarcastic—as an *invitation* being offered to you by someone who is more provoked (in a positive way) by you and more engaged than you might think.

Remember that you are talking with people about a subject that is sensitive. The more that you are perceived as talking *at* them, the more likely they are to think that you are preaching at them and they turn off. Talk *with* them. Get them involved in discussion.

Whatever you do, don't lose your temper. That is never productive.

## Guideline #10: Learn the basics. You have to be a student first before you become a teacher.

Many animal advocates become excited about Abolitionist veganism and the next thing that happens is that they set up a website or start a blog that is motivated by the right feelings but not informed by clear ideas. *Before you teach others, learn the basics.*

This is the most important idea to keep in mind: The Abolitionist Approach is a *grassroots movement.* Advocating veganism as a fundamental principle of justice is not something that requires large, wealthy charities and corporate "leaders." It is something that we can do and *must* do as a grassroots movement. Each one of us must be a leader by educating in a clear and unequivocal way about veganism as a moral imperative and the abolition of exploitation as a fundamental matter of the right of all sentient beings to not be used as things.

But we must each spend the time needed so that we can be effective educators. For example, as we will see in Chapter 6, if we are to be effective in educating people about why it is not necessary to consume animal products for health purposes, we need to know at least the basics about how vegans can satisfy all their nutritional requirements through the consumption of plants.

If we are to be effective educators about Abolitionist veganism as a general matter, we must have at least a basic understanding of Abolitionist theory.

It is also a good idea to be able to understand how to make arguments as a logical matter. In Appendix 2, we discuss ten logical fallacies so that you will better able to spot, and respond to, problematic arguments.

\*\*\*\*\*\*\*\*\*\*

In the next chapter, we discuss *where* to advocate.

# Chapter 2

## Where to Advocate?

The short answer to the question as to where to advocate: *anywhere* and *everywhere*.

We mean that *very* seriously.

You can advocate for veganism in just about *any* situation.

The late Nelson Mandela said that "[e]ducation is the most powerful weapon you can use to change the world." We agree. If you want to change the world, educate, educate, educate, and then educate some more. And education can take place anywhere and in any circumstance.

Always keep in mind, however, that although your advocacy can occur just about anywhere, it should always be nonviolent and respectful; you should always try to engage those you are talking with in creative ways, and you should always make clear that veganism is a moral imperative; it is what we *must* do if we believe that animals matter morally.

Some animal advocates denigrate Abolitionist education and claim it is not "activism." They maintain that it's only "activist" if it involves disruption, confrontation, or street theater. We think creative, nonviolent vegan advocacy is *the* most "activist" thing you can do for nonhuman animals.

In this chapter, we discuss various contexts in which you can advocate. In the next chapter, we will meet some Abolitionist vegan advocates from different countries who will share their advocacy experiences in these and other contexts.

## Never Underestimate the Importance of Communicating with Friends and Acquaintances

It is imperative never to underestimate the importance of talking with friends and acquaintances. Remember what we said in the Introduction: if everyone educated just one other person in a year to go vegan, we could have a vegan world in no time. So if all you did was talk with friends and acquaintances, but you persuaded at least one other person in the next year to go vegan, you'd be doing your part in bringing about the vegan revolution. We only wish that other animal advocates were doing that as well!

Importantly, conversations with friends and acquaintances have the advantage of presenting easier opportunities for follow-up and further engagement. And when you convince a friend or acquaintance to go vegan, that person will most likely influence others. They may do so through discussions with their friends or acquaintances, or they may become involved on a different level and start addressing large groups or going into schools. So you never know what effect you will have in your one-on-one discussions.

You should also never underestimate the one-on-one contacts and conversations that occur with strangers. For example, if you are checking out at a grocery store, with your basket full of fruits and vegetables, that might trigger a comment and start a conversation. Similarly, being in a veterinary office may trigger a discussion about why we love some animals but eat others. We have both had interesting discussions about veganism in supermarkets and vet's offices.

We always carry cards (the size of business cards) that have our website, www.howdoigovegan.com, printed on them. This allows us, in a brief exchange, to provide someone with an excellent "one stop" for all things vegan. Our site contains information on ethics and nutrition, as well as a wide selection of easy and cheap recipes. Abolitionist vegans are available to answer questions online.

## Opportunities for Vegan Advocacy Arise Every Day

Gary was in a video store. The owner of the store was asking another customer about whether she had liked a film that he had recommended. She replied that, although she liked the movie, she was a vegetarian and she was put off by a scene in which a pig was slaughtered. Gary, who was standing nearby, approached the counter and excused himself for interrupting but asked the woman why she was a vegetarian and not a vegan. They spent some time talking and he provided her with the www.howdoigovegan.com URL. She emailed him, thanking him for getting her to think about veganism. Will she go vegan? Maybe. The point is that everyday life provides many opportunities to talk about veganism—even with complete strangers. Some of those people will go vegan. And we will never know who that will be. So we should talk with everyone we can.

Similarly, Anna was at a grocery store recently and asked the person in the bakery whether a particular bread was vegan. Another customer who overheard the question asked Anna what would be in bread that was not vegan. Anna explained that animal ingredients, such as milk, honey, and eggs can be in bread, and that egg wash is sometimes used to give bread a shiny appearance. The woman then spoke with Anna for a while. Anna gave her the website link and referred her to some recipe sites, and about two weeks later, we heard from her that she had gone vegan and wanted to know about where to get non-leather shoes.

Every single day presents opportunities for engaging in creative, non-violent vegan advocacy. Whether you are in a store, a vet's office—*anywhere*—you can almost always get a word in about veganism. In Chapter 5, we talk about a discussion we had at a vet's office. Think about it: people are at the vet's office usually because they love their nonhuman companion. What better place for raising the point that there is no difference between the animals we love and the animals we eat?

If you wear t-shirts or other clothing that has text printed on them, wear something with a vegan message rather than promoting a sports team or rock band. If you carry a bag that has a slogan or information on it, carry one that says something like, "I'm vegan." This can help get conversations started. Whatever you do, don't wear clothing or carry items that promote any non-Abolitionist animal charity. Make sure whatever slogan you have is clearly and unequivocally vegan.

## Online Activism

The internet makes possible something that, just a few years ago, was not possible: people all over the world can communicate directly with other people and have conversations with large numbers of people who share interests, all for the cost of a computer connection. And internet advocacy offers important opportunities for advocates who may face physical challenges to participating in other forms of advocacy. You can be anywhere and travel the world online even if you are unable to leave your home. People who have grown up with the internet often do not understand how profound this is.

Before the advent of the internet, communication about animal issues was largely controlled by the large animal groups. These groups had newsletters and magazines, and they either held conferences and other events, or they participated in one of the large "umbrella" conferences that involved a number of groups. There were several magazines that purported to discuss animal issues but they reflected the positions of the large charities. It was difficult, if not impossible, to get views critical of the corporate charities printed in those magazines. These animal charities controlled communication amongst animal advocates. If those groups did not like the views held by someone, they could, in effect, suppress those views.

The large corporate charities have always been hostile to the Abolitionist movement. If the internet had not come along, things would have stayed exactly the way they were in the 1990s: the "movement" would still be the large corporate charities that promoted welfare reform and single-issue campaigns, and that rejected veganism as a hard-and-fast moral requirement. Although that is exactly what the organized movement is today at the level of the corporate charities, the difference is that there is now an Abolitionist movement—*and it could not have happened without the internet.* There are now people all over the world who embrace the idea that veganism is a moral imperative. And they are busy talking with other people. That is a good thing.

But even if you enjoy meeting people and talking with them, there is nothing wrong with allocating some of your time to online communication. You can reach *thousands* of people in a very short time.

So don't underestimate the power of the internet and its use as a tool to educate others. It is certainly true that the internet has been a very mixed blessing in that, in addition to promoting violence, including misogyny, sexism, racism, and all sorts of hate speech, the internet has encouraged many interested in animal ethics to believe that "activism" is a matter of signing petitions that promote welfare reform or single-issue campaigns. And, of course, the corporate charities have found the internet invaluable as a fundraising tool.

But the problem here is not the internet—the problem is with the welfarist message. The internet has promoted and facilitated the illusion that signing useless petitions and donating to bloated and often corrupt corporate charities that perpetuate animal exploitation are forms of activism. But that was also occurring before the internet showed up. The internet just allows welfarists to spread their message more easily. But if those who are concerned about animal ethics were better educated about matters, the appeal of corporate welfarists would be reduced. And that's where *you* come in!

There are some so-called "animal advocates" who appear to sit on the internet 24 hours a day, 7 days a week, telling Abolitionists that they're not real "activists" because internet education is not activism. Putting aside the irony of people using the internet to declare that communicating on the internet is useless, their claim that internet advocacy is not "real" advocacy is absurd. *There is no difference between educating people using the internet and educating them in any other context.* Using the internet does not make you less of an Abolitionist vegan educator than if you were expressing that same message tabling, speaking to a large audience of people, or engaging in an Abolitionist demonstration.

Internet advocacy offers a wide variety of options: web sites, social media sites, blogs, videos, etc. You can do podcasts. You can write essays and editorials for one of the many online publications. The opportunities are, literally, without limit.

So, if you want to start a blog, or a page, or Facebook discussion group, or you want to do podcasts or YouTube videos so that you can promote Abolitionist veganism, do it. Your work can focus on Abolitionist veganism generally, or your primary focus can be on something else—for example, low-cost, easy, and fast vegan recipes—and you can discuss Abolitionist veganism as part of your presentation.

There are many sites that have an endless need for good content. Contact one of these sites and offer to do an essay on Abolitionist veganism for them.

You may also want to participate on the pages of others who don't promote Abolitionist veganism and challenge them. Indeed, challenging those who promote welfare reform, single-issue campaigns, reducetarianism, etc. is a very valuable activity. Come armed with enthusiasm and well-thought out and well-presented comments and you may convince the people with whom you are interacting that they need to rethink things, and, even if you don't succeed in getting them to think (for many "advocates," it is about business and not ideology), you will still educate the many people who read these pages.

But whatever form your communication takes, always conduct yourself in a creative, nonviolent way. The internet is a violent place. Those who disagree with the Abolitionist Approach, including welfarists and others who reject veganism as a moral baseline, can be very aggressive and they will most certainly attack you in ad hominem ways. Don't take the bait! If people get abusive with you, don't get abusive back. Follow the rules that we outlined in Chapter 1. Educate yourself before you go out and try to educate others. Be clear and unequivocal in promoting veganism as a moral imperative, but don't react or lose your temper. Keep to your creative, nonviolent approach.

## Newspaper Editorials

There are many newspapers, and all of them have online versions. Write an editorial for one these publications.

Most of them have guidelines for submission and rarely consider anything that does not comply with them. Consult those guidelines and tailor your submission for each publication.

## Reading/Study Groups

Another excellent advocacy tool is a reading/study group. Reading/study groups either involve personal meetings or are arranged online with various platforms, some of which are free, and that allow a number of people to participate in group discussion simultaneously. The idea of such a group is to have the members of the group read particular materials and then to discuss those materials. These groups can focus on a single item—a book, essay, or blog post—or they can be more involved and be similar to a sort of course or seminar. They can continue for shorter or longer time periods. For example, there have been a number of reading/study groups that have focused on a particular essay on the www.abolitionistapproach.com website, and that have involved only one or two sessions. There have been groups that have focused on *Animal*

*Rights: The Abolitionist Approach* or *Eat Like You Care* that continue for five or more sessions.

Whatever the extent or focus of a reading group, the idea is the same: to get people together, whether in person or on a platform, which allows them to interact in real time so that the participants can discuss certain, pre-set readings or topics.

## Tabling

Although online advocacy allows you to reach a potentially huge audience, it lacks the dimension of personal interaction, which is an important element in the educational process. Tabling enables such personal engagement.

Is personal interaction more effective than online advocacy?

It's impossible to make generalizations because the effectiveness of communication depends on so many variables. But it is clear that for some people, personal contact is key. For example, having a table with information about veganism and animal rights might well attract that person who would not otherwise be inclined to be searching for information on veganism on the internet. We all know that most "animal lovers" are not vegan. Those people are not likely to be looking for information about veganism. But if they are walking around a market area or other public space, and they see a table that offers information about animals, they might well stop by and provide you with a wonderful opportunity to educate them about why "loving" animals means, in addition to other things, not harming them.

Keep these three things in mind when you table:

*First,* make sure that you have whatever permission you require to set up your table. In many places, you cannot simply set up a table and start talking with people. You may need a permit or you may need to register with some authority or other. Some advocates contact local businesses and get permission to come onto their premises and table.

*Second,* create a table that is attractive and that will make people want to stop and engage. Different advocates have different approaches. Some try to get "animal lovers" to come over and then talk with them about how loving animals is inconsistent with eating, wearing, or using them. For example, we know one advocate who tables using a banner that says, "Do You Love Animals?" As soon as someone approaches, the advocate initiates a discussion about veganism. Others explicitly make veganism a central part of the invitation.

*Third,* a very effective form of advocacy involves giving away samples of vegan food. This helps to dispel the notion that vegans consume substances that are strange and unappetizing. So having cupcakes, cookies, and other food samples can be an easy way to get people into a discussion.

Some places require approval by a health department or similar regulatory body before food can be distributed. Other places impose restrictions only if food is sold. But in all cases, you should be sure to disclose ingredients so that anyone with an allergy or other sensitivity can avoid what you are offering.

## Advocating Over Food

A big part of vegan advocacy is getting people to see that vegan food is not only nothing to be scared of, but is downright delicious. Indeed, many a decision to go vegan began with enjoying some vegan food.

You can provide some vegan food to people as part of your tabling, or vegan food can take a more central role. That is, you can have events where you invite those who are interested in learning about veganism to come to a vegan pot luck dinner where they can discuss veganism with Abolitionists.

## Advocating in Art and Music

Do you have artistic or musical talent?

If you do, put it to work for the animals! You can express Abolitionist vegan messages in art and in your songs.

## Talks at Local Public Spaces, Schools, Colleges, Universities

If you are willing to speak publicly to groups about animal ethics, you will find no end of opportunities. Community groups, animal groups, environmental groups, schools, colleges, and universities, and student organizations at educational facilities, are always on the lookout for speakers. Many primary (grammar) schools are reluctant to have someone come in who wants to promote veganism (as opposed to "kind treatment") to younger children. But secondary (high) schools are often interested in Abolitionist speakers.

You should contact local groups and let them know that you are available to come to talk about veganism. A good place to start is with your local college or university. Ask them for contact information for campus animal groups. Some of these groups will not want you to speak because they promote new welfarist perspectives. Indeed, a number of student groups have formal ties of one sort or another with the large corporate groups. But many student groups will welcome you and some may even want you to debate with welfarists who reject veganism as a moral imperative. These are excellent opportunities to educate.

## Getting Abolitionist Materials into Libraries

We have sent copies of books we have written to community libraries and to high school libraries so that people can be exposed to Abolitionist thinking. You can do the same in your community.

To the extent that libraries have said that the material is too "radical," we have pointed out that their collections contain a great deal of material that encourages animal exploitation, and that Abolitionist materials help to balance the perspective on the morality of animal use.

## Marches, Demonstrations, Street Theater, etc.

What about marches, demonstrations, or street theater? Or what about *any* form of advocacy other than the ones we have discussed above?

The answer is always the same: if it is nonviolent and engages people in a creative way, and if it involves being crystal clear about veganism as a moral imperative—then go for it. If not, then don't.

The main problem with marches and demonstrations is that, for the most part, they are not clearly Abolitionist. Indeed, most are welfarist, promote single-issue campaigns, or are otherwise not Abolitionist. For example, a "march against slaughterhouses" gives the impression that the problem is meat, and the suppliers of meat. In fact, the problem is all animal products and all of the consumers who demand those animal products.

Events where animal advocates stop trucks carrying animals to slaughter so that they can "witness" the exploitation, or offer comfort to the animals, are problematic in large part because the animals are in a horrible state of distress already and stopping the trucks so that advocates can "bear witness" does nothing more than increase that distress. Advocates often stick their arms into the trucks to offer water to the animals and to take photos. This does not help the animals. Advocates are often very emotional during these events. This does not help the animals either. Many of these events do not in any way convey a clear vegan message.

Much "activism" is really nothing more than street theater that is not Abolitionist in that it focuses on issues of treatment and not use and does not promote a clear message that veganism is a moral imperative. Indeed, some of those who promote this sort of advocacy go out of their way not to talk about veganism. Some of these groups claim to promote veganism in their street theater, but they also promote, and may even do events with, the large corporate welfarist charities, and thereby send out a very confused message. Moreover, much of this street theater involves other problems, such as sexist displays.

## A Note About Advocacy in the Workplace

A cautionary point: Many employers prohibit promoting ethical or political positions in the workplace. So be careful so that you don't lose your job!

To the extent you can advocate in your workplace, follow the principles you would follow in any other context. Be simple and straight-forward. Aim to present a consistent message and use care that you don't upset co-workers or aggravate your supervisor. Your goal should be to introduce veganism in a friendly way that will invite questions and create the desire for additional information. You may have a vegan tea mug or calendar at your desk, some photos of your nonhuman companions and perhaps some printed thoughts about veganism posted in your space to generate curiosity. Everyone likes a treat so share some home-baked cookies or other vegan goodies with your co-workers. Have a copy of the recipe handy and explain the ingredients. Tell them about the www.howdoigovegan.com website, where they may find additional recipes and information about veganism. Keep a copy of *Eat Like You Care: An Examination of the Morality of Eating Animals,* so you can lend it to your workmates. Once the door is open, advocating at work is really no different than anywhere else as long as you remember to maintain professionalism and don't allow your efforts to interfere with your work.

## A Note About the Use of Graphic or Violent Imagery— Slaughterhouse Footage, etc.

People always ask us why we don't use graphic imagery in our work. The answer is simple: animal use is taken by most as a given. That is because our conventional wisdom about animals is that it is morally acceptable to use animals as long as we treat them "humanely." That's what the overwhelming number of people believe. When people see violent imagery involving animal use, their minds go immediately to: "that's terrible; they ought to make those abuses illegal and make sure the animals are treated properly."

Moreover, the use of graphic imagery often prompts people to make a donation because, as a psychological matter, they want whatever horrible situation they are looking at to be rectified somehow. They aren't giving any thought as to how to address the problem in a systematic way.

That is why all of the large animal charities use violent imagery: it generates support for welfarist campaigns and single-issue campaigns, and reinforces the idea that the problem is the treatment of animals and the goal is to seek more "humane" exploitation.

For Abolitionist veganism to become the paradigm, we need to focus on one simple idea: animal exploitation—however supposedly "humane"—is unjust, unfair, and wrong. Abolitionists are not looking for donations. They want one thing: for people to go vegan.

\*\*\*\*\*\*\*\*\*\*

In the next chapter, we will meet some Abolitionist vegan advocates who do the sorts of advocacy and education we have discussed in this chapter.

# Chapter 3

## Reflections and Ideas from Some Abolitionist Vegan Advocates

In this chapter, we will present some reflections and ideas from Abolitionist vegan advocates from all over the world. These are all *grassroots* advocates. They do not belong to, work with, or support any of the large animal welfare charities.

We will consider some suggestions from Abolitionist vegans who do tabling, reading/study groups, and food events. In the final section, we will consider a set of tried and true ideas from Abolitionist vegan advocates from around the world.

### Tabling

There are many Abolitionists who table and we have chosen four—Elizabeth Collins of New Zealand, Vanda Kadas in California, Andreas Månsson of Sweden and Peggy Warren of Washington State in the United States—to provide a brief description of their efforts. Several other Abolitionist vegan advocates also focused on tabling at the presentations that they did at The World Vegan Summit and these comments will appear in the final section.

### Elizabeth Collins, New Zealand:

I table in Auckland New Zealand and have been doing it for almost eight years. I started very small with a fold-up table with which I travelled by bus. I now have a car and can more easily transport my materials, which include a larger table and food (usually cupcakes). I usually have one or two people who work with me. Here are the practical steps I followed and some thoughts:

I wrote to the Auckland Council and asked if I could get permission to do this in Auckland. I have been approached by officials several times and as soon as I showed them my street trader license they were satisfied and left me alone. I was granted permission to set up my table in three places. One of these was the prime spot in Auckland for all activities, right by Aotea Square, so that is the location I always go to. I also go to markets and festivals at various locations in the city.

I have a table, and a big eye-catching banner hanging along the front of the table that says "Stop Violence. Go Vegan." I also have some other Abolitionist-themed posters I hang from the sides, so people coming from the side see something. I have messages on the table such as "Veganism = Respect and Nonviolence." These are all conversation-starters. I have a range of books and materials written by Gary Francione and Anna Charlton, and I also have business cards for the website www.howdoigovegan.com as well as Abolitionist pamphlets, recipe booklets, "vegan passports" (information about where visitors can get vegan food) and cupcakes with a sign saying, "Free Cupcakes With Conversation."

A lot of people come over and inquire what we're doing, or they make a comment or have a question about one of the messages on the posters. Or they come looking for vegan recipes and other information. Or they come to argue or to try to make a point. We go from there.

In the beginning, in 2009, I never met any vegans at all, and mostly people were asking me what on earth "vegan" was when I mentioned it to them. At first I didn't have the word prominently displayed; now that word dominates. People look for advice and guidance on how to go vegan; they come over because they have family members who are vegan and want to find out more about it, or want to get recipes to cook for them. Mostly people come over to talk, and usually about welfare—

about treating animals more "humanely." Once we start talking about the Abolitionist Approach, the conversation gets deep but it gets simpler and less complicated than conversations about treatment. You can see the light bulbs going on in people's eyes; you can see their minds absorbing the concepts. It's a beautiful thing.

I think once people start doing an Abolitionist stall and don't use graphic imagery, then they are setting a platform for an amazing experience. It is great practice and a wonderful way for advocates to clarify their own thoughts and build their own voices and advocacy style. Unlike how the animal movement has portrayed this for decades, it doesn't have to be about shouting and anger and yelling and confrontation. It shouldn't only be one-way activism out there: chanting at people, yelling at people, holding signs in mute protest, showing videos to people. We must engage *with* people. And those who do, and who are armed with Abolitionist theory, can attest to how effective and amazing it is.

The negative experiences? They vary, and are outweighed by the positive by a long shot, but for me personally the most negative are the "plants are sentient" crowd. So annoying!

### Vanda Kadas, United States and Hungary:

I have been a vegan for more than 20 years, and have always spoken with people around me (and online) about the importance of going vegan. I have made it a point to table in more economically challenged areas because I reject the idea that veganism is in any way "elitist." I also think it's very important to bring the vegan message to areas where many just assume that there will be little interest. I do most of my tabling in and around East Palo Alto in California. I table regularly with colleagues and we reach hundreds of people each time.

The interest in veganism in the areas in which I table has been phenomenal! People are full of questions, full of empathy, and they say things like, "never thought about things this way before!" Many people have decided to become vegan as a result of conversations at the table. People wanted to know all about how to do right by the animals while doing right by their limited food budget too. It was heartwarming to witness when people really got the idea that unless we are vegan we keep sending animals to slaughter, completely unnecessarily.

I am also interested in educating children about veganism as the moral baseline. The key here is to be honest without being graphic. I

43

sincerely believe most of us see the importance of veganism at a young age before social conditioning clouds up our existing beliefs. I have never heard a child say, "yay! that's great—they killed a chicken so now we can have chicken soup." Most, if not all, children become sincerely concerned when we tell them exactly how the bodies of animals, or their secretions, ended up on our plate. Since the sense of fairness is acute in young children, the Abolitionist Approach once again supports our dialogue with children too. I most often employ a question-based advocacy style with young children, and I ask short, simple, direct questions, such as "if we bite into an apple is the apple going to cry?" "Why not?" "How about if we were to bite into a cat, would she cry?" "Why?" The children are learning the concepts of *sentience*, the fact that plants are not sentient beings and the fair thing is to become a vegan so we don't purposely harm another sentient being.

We also have "Vegan Facts" cards at our table that we created and use mostly with older children and also with adults occasionally. The cards provide facts about veganism, which are great conversation openers. For example, one card says: "How many animals do we slaughter annually?" This approach gets us into discussion immediately. Interestingly, children inspire their parents to take up an interest in veganism.

I wholeheartedly believe we need to educate ourselves before we go out and educate others. The Abolitionist Approach is easy to learn and to follow. Even more importantly: it is necessary to be well-versed in a solid animal rights theory so we can be as rationally convincing as possible when educating people from all walks of life.

### Andreas Månsson, Sweden:

Tabling is one of the most potent forms of vegan advocacy one can do as an Abolitionist on a grassroots level. When you are promoting the Abolitionist Approach and the Six Principles, you are going to notice that vegan education *differs* from the way non-Abolitionist advocates—welfarists—do it. Actually, the approach is quite the opposite.

Abolitionist vegans ask reflective questions of ourselves, such as *why*, *when* and *how* we advocate. The vegan message is clear, unequivocal and nonviolent. Veganism is an imperative; the default position.

How we talk to the public in our communities (or more importantly how the public approaches and talks to us) in one-on-one conversations also reveals a lot about how attractive the vegan message is that we try to convey.

Here are some tips on vegan tabling:

1.  People are good at heart, care morally about animals and don't want to inflict unnecessary suffering upon them. Every person you meet is a potential vegan.

2.  Make vegan tabling a routine in your daily life, plan ahead and try to do it consistently.

3.  Take advantage of the free resources from the Abolitionist Approach website and use them exclusively. For example, the Abolitionist Approach pamphlet is currently translated into 28 languages. Use the material carefully and respect the importance of the content.

4.  Don't have too many items on your table. You should include pamphlets, a couple of books (such as *Eat Like You Care*), a sheet for collecting contact details, and maybe some vegan cookies.

5.  Listen and be interested in the person who approaches you, but always focus on veganism as the moral baseline and also *ask* questions.

6.  Set goals in your advocacy. Reflect and evaluate. How did you frame the conversation? What were the weaknesses / strengths in your arguments? Educate yourself through Professor Francione's books, essays, podcasts and other materials.

7.  Reject animal organizations, branding, memberships, economic donations or selling merchandise like t-shirts, buttons, tote bags and more.

8.  Don't use violent imagery.

9.  Avoid speciesist language.

10. Let the public in your community borrow books from you. This has at least two purposes:

    a. Nonvegans can educate themselves and critically reflect about veganism as an imperative;

    b. You can inspire vegans in your community and offer them

the opportunity to join an Abolitionist reading group in animal rights theory and learn more about Professor Francione's work.

11. Do follow-ups.

**Peggy Warren, United States:**

I usually table at the local State college where permits aren't required for non-commercial stands. I set up in front of a building with high foot-traffic at a time when students are more likely to be.

For portability, I use a compact, sturdy collapsible hand truck to carry my equipment—a small folding table, a collapsible chair, a large "GO VEGAN" banner and mount—from the parking lot. I also bring a table cloth, a range of Abolitionist Approach outreach materials and books, and some vegan treats.

When people approach the table, I greet them with a friendly "Hi" and a big smile, and ask if they are considering going vegan. Then I focus on listening to them so I can answer questions, and try to elicit their thoughts and concerns about animals. By focusing on animal use and on veganism as the least we can do, people can rapidly come to the realization that, once they've acknowledged their moral concern, nothing short of veganism can fulfill their moral obligation to animals. I try to be firm, consistent, helpful and honest about my own struggles.

It is important to remember that tabling is something that gets easier with practice. Every time you go out you may encounter people who challenge you and don't seem to hear you, but you also meet many, many people who are genuinely thrilled you are there to answer their questions and help them understand veganism and go vegan.

The high point of my last tabling day was meeting a man who has a 13-year-old daughter who went vegan because, in his words, "she just can't stand the thought of continuing to harm animals." He told me she was leading the way to convince him, their entire household and even the extended family to go vegan. This man was eager to educate himself in order to support her and to learn how to vegan himself. He was so excited and thankful that I was there to supply him with information and answer his questions. I thanked him right back and said his story totally made my day.

There are people everywhere who are eager to learn about veganism.

All we need to do is reach out to connect with them. The world is vegan! If you want it.

## Reading/Study Groups

Reading/study groups can take a number of forms. They can go on for a period of weeks or months and be structured like seminars where there are one or more people who lead the group, which consists of individuals who commit to participate for the length of the seminar. The group meets and discusses readings that are assigned beforehand. Another model is to have more informal meetings where particular topics are discussed and where people show up at one session but not necessarily at another, and where there may or may not be assigned reading beforehand. All such groups can be done in person or online.

An example of an Abolitionist group that uses the more formal model is the International Vegan Association (www.internationalvegan.org), which, in addition to other projects it pursues, offers both online and in-person reading groups in which participants meet to discuss animal ethics and read materials from the history of philosophy, going back to ancient times and continuing through to the present day, and more informal discussion groups. More informal (but very effective) models are followed by Veganos pela Abolição (Vegans for Abolition) (www.veganospelaabolicao.org/animal/) a grassroots group in Brazil, Abolisyonist Vegan Hareket (Abolitionist Vegan Movement) (http://abolisyonistveganhareket.org/) in Turkey. These descriptions were written by the advocates themselves.

### International Vegan Association (USA and Canada)
### Dave Langlois:

The International Vegan Association (IVA) is a small, exclusively volunteer-operated organization based in the United States, but supporting grassroots abolitionist advocates worldwide. Although the IVA is a legally incorporated charitable group, it does not solicit or accept donations from the general public.

The IVA's purpose is to help grassroots advocates do their own, independent abolitionist educational work across the globe.

The IVA runs "train-the-trainer"-style reading and discussion workshops, both online and in person. These workshops give educators the chance to do a deep dive on core issues in ethical theory, animal rights philosophy, the history of the animal advocacy movement, the welfare-Abolition debate, and current issues in abolitionist methodology. The point of these groups is to make advocates more comfortable and confident in their own educational initiatives, and to empower them to run their own reading and discussion workshops.

In addition to the reading groups, the IVA produces digital and print resources that advocates can use in their work, including a full-color 28-page Vegan Starter Kit (featuring Abolitionist moral arguments, a comprehensive nutrition guide, and recipes). Abolitionists from across the world can apply to receive a shipment of these Kits right to their door, free of charge, for use in their advocacy.

Finally, the IVA occasionally releases "think tank"-like position papers on topics in Abolitionist theory and practice. Covering topics like movement strategy, whether Abolitionists should form groups, and why consuming even trace quantities of animal-based ingredients is morally problematic, these papers are another supportive educational tool for abolitionist advocates.

### Vegans for Abolition (Brazil)
### Vera R. Cristofani and Luís Martini:

GEFRAN, which stands for Grupo de Estudos da Teoria de Gary Francione, or, in English, Study Group on Gary Francione's Theory, is a reading group that is one of the projects of Veganos pela Abolição (Vegans for Abolition), a grassroots group in São Paulo, Brazil. We created GEFRAN after realizing that vegans and nonvegans should have more access to good information about, and good training in, animal rights and Abolitionist theory.

The first GEFRAN meeting was held on April 17, 2010 at a vegan restaurant in São Paulo. From the beginning of the Group until today, the theme of the meetings is based directly on the work of Gary Francione and Anna Charlton. We often investigate and analyze various campaigns promoted by the large animal groups in light of Abolitionist theory.

Meetings are open to the general public and are free of charge. They happen once a month, on Saturday afternoons and last about three hours. Currently, they take place at the vegan restaurant Lar Vegan in São Paulo. GEFRAN does not have the format of a traditional academic class as it has to adapt to the reality of random participants. The theoretical development of the theme is mainly under the responsibility of a person who serves as facilitator of the particular meeting. The facilitator prepares the topic and does a presentation to the group, although we usually post materials online for people to read beforehand. On occasion, we may invite people who have a particular expertise in a topic to speak or facilitate.

One of our goals is to train people so that they become more active and able Abolitionist educators in terms of their communicating with the general public. In turn, they may help to train additional educators by having sessions with others similar to what we provide. In this way, more and more people become aware of the moral and inherent value of nonhuman animals. They become aware of the problem of speciesism and the solution—Abolitionist veganism.

### Abolitionist Vegan Movement (Turkey)
### Gülce Özen Gürkan and Berk Efe Altinal:

We engage in community-based education with vegans who are familiar with the Abolitionist Approach and who already actively advocate for veganism. We meet on a regular basis at a set time, and, for each session, someone volunteers to do a presentation of about 30 minutes in length. Reading material may be circulated in advance, then the speaker presents the topic and we ask questions and discuss the topic. A moderator, chosen from within the group, keeps the discussion moving along.

We have a social media group exclusively for the communication of the meetings and the meeting notes. We also make audio recordings of the meetings but these are only for archival purposes, and we discourage people from listening to recordings rather than coming and attending the actual sessions.

So far, this project has gone very well. A byproduct of these meetings is that many of us have become more confident about advocating for veganism and abolitionist veganism. These meetings are one of the most fruitful education experiences we, as the organizers, have experienced.

## Advocating Over Food: Vegan Potlucks

Gülce Özen Gürkan and Berk Efe Altinal of Turkey also have weekly meetings where Abolitionists share the labor and prepare food (the members of the group each prepare a dish) and anyone who is interested in learning about veganism can come and share a meal. During the meal, the Abolitionist hosts talk with their guests about veganism. So they are advocating at a vegan dinner that they put on. This is a *very* effective way of educating people. This following was written by Gülce and Efe:

"Vegan potlucks are open to both vegans and nonvegans. We encourage vegans to bring their nonvegan friends and family members with them. Every vegan brings some food, preferably homemade (to share some recipes) but at least some fruits or nuts, or some good vegan food bought from a restaurant. We don't expect nonvegans to bring food in their first attendance, but if they leave the potluck still not convinced to go vegan, we expect them to bring some vegan food next time so they can see it's at least as easy as preparing something nonvegan. The potlucks are moderated by Abolitionist vegans. Our priority is talking to nonvegans on veganism as a moral imperative, and as something very easy to do. We always bring pamphlets with us and give them to the nonvegans so they have something to read and think about after they leave. Many nonvegans just go vegan after joining one potluck.

It's very important to keep the potlucks regular, so we do it on a weekly basis not only to make it routine in our lives but to be able to offer it as a regular source of support and information to those who are new vegans or aspiring to veganism. During the winter, we use a house owned by a vegan who lets us use the facility. When it's warm again, we do the potlucks in open public spaces like parks or sea sides. We announce every potluck in social media; they are generally on the same day of the week and the same hour of the day. Organising the potlucks in a very cosmopolitan city, we have a safe-space policy which clearly states that discriminatory and violent behaviors or attitudes are not welcome."

## Some More Ideas

Abolitionist vegan advocates are speaking out for animals all around the world. Here are some more of their ideas for grassroots advocacy. For the most part, these statements were parts of presentations made at the World Vegan Summit, which was organized by Bob Linden (www. goveganradio.com) and took place at the University of California at Berkeley in 2016.

### *Activist Tip: Avoid Going Blue*
**Sue Coe, United States and England:**

To see directly the content with my own eyes is paramount, whether a slaughterhouse or prison, laboratory or animal rescue. If I cannot gain access, that itself becomes the story: what is being concealed and why? My art work is about looking through my eyes, not looking into my eyes and noting they are blue. The forensic research element is important, but I place that research in mental storage to retrieve when necessary, as I have discovered that facts rarely move anyone to change, but they are necessary building blocks to building the case.

People engage emotionally before they seek the facts. If I speak of "climate change" or how many animals are rendered into products for human consumption, it has the flavor of something inevitable; that creates a passive hopelessness. But if this is phrased in a different way—as a symptom, not the disease—people understand. It is as if we are describing witnessing someone being murdered and we notice the body is turning blue, and then conclude that the color blue should be banned to resolve the problem. Or if we describe how animals are exsanguinated on the kill floor in a slaughterhouse, and the solution is to ban the color red. If the murder is described as the very murder of the planet from the view of a horizontal intruder—a poet, or musician, or artist—it has a unique perspective that engages people. Art is an antidote to digital psychosis. It slows time down. Art doesn't become art until the viewer has made it so, translated through their own unique vision. Nonhuman animals perceive the world not from the isolating and individual view of power, control, ownership and naming, but in a radical inclusive way. Animals own not one blade of grass, or one drop of water, one gulp of air, or one leaf on a tree, yet they feel a part of all those elements and value their freedom above all.

To expose the disease, not the symptom, is to address the crime of capitalism, which puts profit before all life. We are trained to sleep through capitalism, accept it as inevitable, and not wake up and demand another world—a world that values life before profit.

When I describe going into a slaughterhouse, in words and art, I am re-traumatizing others. Animal activists feel so sad, sometimes despairing, and are isolated because witnessing the cruelty inflicted on animals is like acid thrown onto an etching plate; it cuts deep, yet acid is colorless, invisible, but when that plate is printed and the ink reveals the deep cuts and is then printed onto paper, others can see. The injustice becomes visible, and once seen it can be changed. Animal rights is a social justice movement akin to any other social justice movement in history.

Becoming a vegan is the very least we can do to help animals. Farmed animals are being bred only to be murdered, oceans are being emptied of aquatic life, animals suffer in their billions—a suffering that is almost incomprehensible in its enormity. It is a serious discussion that requires that we either go into a slaughterhouse or mentally go into a slaughterhouse to understand our complicity and our silence. I use the Abolitionist Approach because it works. It's simple and it's elegant, and it is black and white, and I like black and white, in art, and everything else—it does the job. It empowers people with a vision. We have the power to stop this appalling destruction of life today, to make the bold step; it doesn't need manipulation or money or access to power.

Even if we are alone and know no other vegans, we still can join the global movement of nonviolence, which is growing larger by the minute. My activist tip, is this: after we have discussed going vegan, and debated and discussed, and people are convinced they can do this, as a positive first step, I then ask, "who is not going vegan?" A few people will raise their hands. I respond that my lifelong mission to help animals means everything to me, and I have failed the animals if people are not going vegan. Can they please explain how I can improve? How they can help me to convince them? Have I missed something in my presentation? What can I do better? The answers have been very good. I have learned so much by asking these questions, as they include everyone as important forces in the revolution for animals; no one is left out.

### *Use Language Carefully*
**Cristina Cubells, Spain:**

The so-called "animal movement" today is not Abolitionist.

All large animal organizations reject veganism as a moral baseline and they confuse people about the morality of using animals. As a general matter, they don't talk about veganism and when they do, they discuss it as a "lifestyle" or as a way to reduce the suffering of animals. They promote animal welfare reforms and single-issue campaigns. Far from helping animals, these advocates validate their exploitation, reinforce speciesism, and send very problematic messages that make advocating for animals more complicated.

Unfortunately, we cannot stop this from happening.

But there is something that we can and *must* do. We can advocate for animals with a clear and unambiguously Abolitionist message: *using animals is wrong, regardless of how we treat them.*

In order to do that, it is very important to be careful with the language we use. We must make sure that we are promoting a coherent and consistent animal rights position. The difference between a confusing message and a clear message can lead to terrible consequences for animals. Here are some examples of confusing language:

*"Against animal cruelty"*: This is a concept widely used by animal organizations. The concept of "animal cruelty" does not question the *use* of animals itself, but puts the focus of attention on *treatment*, and it validates the idea that there could be a good way to use animals. There isn't: *all* use is wrong and must be rejected.

*"Veg"/ "Vegetarian"/ "Veggie"*: Many people use the words "vegetarian," "veg," "veggie," etc., in order to avoid using "vegan." This is problematic because we are validating the idea that something less than veganism is a morally acceptable option. It isn't. If animals matter morally, veganism is the only choice. In order to promote it, we must use the word "vegan" and there's nothing wrong in doing so. We actually *need* to talk about veganism if we want people to understand why they must go vegan!

*"Carnists"/ "Meat-eaters"*: The use of these terms implies that the consumption of meat is morally different from the consumption of other animal products and, consequently, it promotes the idea that vegetarianism is an acceptable option.

*"Compassion"/ "Pity"/ "Mercy"*: All these words involve a feeling of sadness that comes from seeing someone suffering. A movement of justice is not based on what people *feel*, but on the moral obligation to respect others, regardless of their feelings. In the same way that women demand respect from men—and not their compassion, mercy or pity—we should not ask for less than respect for animals. Feeling bad about the suffering of animals is normal, but feelings are not the basis of a movement for justice that seeks the recognition that we cannot morally justify treating other sentient beings as things.

*"100% vegan"*: Using percentages when we speak about veganism implies that there is the possibility of being "50% vegan." This is false, in the same way that it would be wrong to say that someone can be 50% not racist. When we talk about veganism, as Professor Gary Francione says, there are only two options: either you are vegan, or you participate directly in animal exploitation. There is no third choice.

There are other words and concepts that can be confusing. However, in all cases, the idea is always the same: we should employ language that questions the use of animals and avoids anything that could lead to confusion. Take the necessary time with each person to be sure that they have understood the message clearly. Being vegan is easy. So is understanding veganism if we explain it in the right way. Let's educate ourselves in order to be good advocates, and let's not miss a single opportunity to promote veganism. We should always educate in respectful and nonviolent ways, but we must always be clear: *using animals is unfair; being fair with animals means, at a minimum, being vegan.*

## On Graphic Imagery
**Ben Frost, England:**

Our society is founded on two hundred years of animal welfarism, so much so that it has become the default position of almost every nonvegan. Everyone agrees that animals have moral value. But the average nonvegan will also maintain that animal use is justifiable if the nonhuman is treated "humanely." This is welfarism in practice. It permeates the very fabric of our society upon which people form their core moral views.

It is within this context that graphic imagery must be understood and deconstructed.

As a fundamental matter, there is no way for a nonvegan to interpret a graphic image or street stunt (such as showing graphic films on video or laptop screens) other than from their baseline welfarist standpoint. The image or stunt does not challenge their core belief that animal use is acceptable. On the contrary, it reaffirms to them that treatment, and not use, is the central issue. In doing this, it perpetuates the notion that the only fundamental interest nonhumans possess is the interest in not suffering. The graphic image or stunt in itself does not deny the existence of an interest in continued life, but in directing the nonvegans' attention to treatment (as all violent imagery does), it serves to perpetuate that central tenet of animal welfarism: the idea that it's only treatment that matters because the animals we exploit don't have an interest in continuing to live.

There are a number of other issues too, including (but not limited to) the profound disrespect we show nonhumans in using their desecrated bodies in street theatre, or as imagery to shock or entice. We need to take the principle of equal consideration seriously, and not view animals' bodies, or their suffering, as tools in our advocacy arsenal. We would never do so in the human context, and we shouldn't in the animal context. As a practical matter, violent imagery will never be anything but counterproductive. We need to be clear that animal use—regardless of the treatment—is morally unjustifiable. Violent imagery in our advocacy will do nothing but perpetuate the dominant welfarist paradigm. More so than ever, we need clarity, not ambiguity. I often work with my colleague, Jenny Trigg, of Manchester Abolitionist Vegans. We never use graphic imagery and we have had great success in engaging people in discussion and getting them to see the moral imperative of veganism.

## *The Use of Visual Arts in Abolitionist Advocacy*
**Marianna C. Gonzalez, Mexico:**

I'd say that most people who have engaged in online or on-site Abolitionist advocacy have had to make use of visual material in one form or another. Many of us have experienced firsthand how the quality of an image can add value and impact to a written or spoken message, particularly when advocating about Abolitionism. This is why the role of the visual arts in creative and nonviolent Abolitionist vegan advocacy may seem obvious when we consider the frequent use of print-ready or online posters, comics, paintings, drawings, photography etc., and yet it is a means through which the possibilities for creative self-expression in conjunction with the delivery of a clear Abolitionist vegan message are endless and ideal for those with an interest in a form of communication that relies heavily on image-making.

In my view, animal advocates are well advised to consider the following when looking to use their art or design skills as an integral part of their Abolitionist educational efforts.

*First*, I think that making art in the context of Abolitionist advocacy serves three purposes:

1. It allows the advocate with artistic inclinations to satisfy a personal and often deep-seated need for creative expression. To my mind, art making in its essence stems from the joy and pleasure of creating, but in the context of advocacy, this joy is by far heightened with a sense of purpose and urgency to bring justice to nonhuman animals. At a personal level, art making may be fulfilling in itself, but in the context of Abolitionist advocacy, it has a substantive *raison d'être* with which to take form.

2. It oftentimes constitutes a pithy Abolitionist message that

stands on its own when the images in question created to educate or disseminate Abolitionism contain text or are coupled with text. In this sense, the images and text together constitute "bite-size" units of Abolitionist theory meant to be grasped by an audience that is accustomed to receiving information through visual means. It is worth noting that different audiences learn differently and the audience that most benefits from the use of art in advocacy is that which has a preference and facility for learning through images.

3. These same images serve also as an *invitation* to get the viewer to go directly to the source of these ideas and educate themselves on Abolitionist theory. In other words, these visual units of information created for an audience that is visually oriented function as "gateway" material to direct the viewer to the books and essays by Gary Francione and Anna Charlton.

*Second*, and considering the purposes of making art in the context of advocacy mentioned above, in order to create visual images that communicate and educate effectively, I recommend that the artistically inclined advocate pay close attention to the following:

Their own Abolitionist education: The advocate must understand Abolitionist theory in depth in order for them to avoid inadvertently creating images that may be ideologically unclear or simply not in alignment with Abolitionist theory. As Professor Francione often says, you need to be a student before you become a teacher!

Their art/design education as well: I suggest that the advocate endeavor to learn and develop their craft as much as possible, and strive to become the best designer or artist they can be.

Exploring different forms of visual expression: This is related to the previous point but it is worth highlighting: I suggest that the advocate try different artistic styles and materials—materials that are free of animal products, obviously—as doing so will broaden their pictorial vocabulary, make their visual work more interesting and varied, and help them identify the kind of images they most enjoy creating and that are most meaningful to them.

*Third*, the advocate who does visual art could also work with other creative Abolitionist advocates who are interested in music and/or writing in order to create together educational materials that combine other creative skills or artistic expressions. The possibilities could lead to very interesting results.

*Fourth,* as a general matter, my main recommendation to the Abolitionist advocate (artistically inclined or not) is that they channel what they are good at and enjoy doing towards their advocacy. This will make their advocacy richer, more creative and fulfilling for them personally, and ultimately more impactful for those who are ripe to hear an Abolitionist message. Creative, nonviolent Abolitionist advocacy positions us to optimize our talents in the service of justice to nonhuman animals. As I see it, we are morally obligated to use our talents for the benefit of those who are disempowered and exploited—those who need our voices through whichever means they communicate in order to shift the paradigm of animals as property to animals as nonhuman persons.

## Expressing the Message in Song
### Gülce Özen Gürkan, Turkey:

If you're a vegan song-writer, writing songs about animal rights and veganism is a very good way of activism. But it needs a balance of good ethics and good music. You shouldn't make people feel like they're listening to brain-washing accompanied by music. And also, you shouldn't make people feel like you're trying to sell your music using the ideas. If you manage to make people understand that you're just expressing your feelings about the issue via your music, only then can you get the reactions you want.

Remember, your reference point is not the people who already think the same as you, but the nonvegans who decide or consider going vegan after listening to your songs. It is important that you have incorporated the thoughts and feelings into your own life before you try to use a song to reach and touch others. You can't write a song a song that will move people to think about veganism if you are not yourself a vegan who understands veganism as a principle of justice.

You can release your songs in social media, or make an album, or put them into your albums including songs with different themes (this way your song can reach to the hearts softened by the other songs in the album), or sing them or play their recordings in concerts or animal rights events, or during your vegan tabling. After a good vegan talk, the songs can create the moral impulse needed to go vegan. It's better to release your songs with videos. Even a very simple one with lovely animal images is just fine. If your song is heard by many, someone else might randomly make a video of your song with unwanted images or scenes including graphic images of animals. If your song doesn't already have a nice video, people might remember your song with those images and it might decrease the effect of your advocacy.

### *Providing Abolitionist Vegan Education for Children*
**Vanda Kadas, United States and Hungary:**

During our weekly Vegan Tabling Thursdays we are thankful for the many children who stop at our Abolitionist vegan display. We tap into creative vegan advocacy in order to sustain their interest and to foster their vegan education. Our display is purposely colorful, with many fresh fruits, vegetables, wholegrain crackers, spreads, and some sweet treats. We employ many Abolitionist vegan posters, mindfully geared toward children as well, for example. a picture of a cow with her calf, or a human child interacting with a cow. Children get attracted to our vivid display and stay for a game, or just for an interesting and thought-provoking conversation about veganism as the moral baseline.

The watermelon game is one of our popular attractions. I ask the children what will happen if someone cuts a watermelon, and what will happen if someone cuts a pig. Children readily acknowledge that a watermelon, being a plant, has no feelings. On the other hand, pigs will "cry and try to run away" if someone is hurting them. I then point out that since animals hurt and plants do not, we should eat the plants and leave animals alone. Children seem to understand Abolitionist vegan ideas even faster than adults, in my experience!

When children are busy looking at our display and/or helping themselves to some wholesome vegan food we help them understand what veganism means, and why all animal use needs to end. Several children have decided to go vegan and have brought their families around!

Children are particularly open to education, and as such they are good candidates for sensitive and positive vegan advocacy. We need to bring about a vegan world, and we need to do it now. As Professors Francione and Charlton say, "The world is vegan! If you want it."

### *Advocacy Tip: Identify Issues and Keep It Simple*
**Emilia Leese, England and Scotland:**

Whenever I face answering a question about veganism or writing about any aspect of it, I do two things. First, I identify what are the issues and second, as much as possible, I keep it simple.

Identifying the issues is important because it keeps us focused on what is really at stake. Sometimes we get questions that roll many other issues into one. This is because people are overwhelmed by our rejection of something that the vast majority of the world does on a daily basis; at other times, questions that conflate issues may come from fellow vegans.

Three examples come to mind, two of which I have written about before for *Ecorazzi*. The first is the conflation of poverty and veganism (https://goo.gl/vBJ1tb) that is, veganism as an obligation versus income inequality/poverty as the "impossibility" to going vegan. These are two separate issues and they should be addressed separately. Sure, there are relationships between these issues, but that does not mean that one negates the other.

The second is when we hear people talking about veganism as a journey. (https://goo.gl/zs7MLw). *We* all went vegan as a result of some experience, but veganism is not about us. "We" are not the focus of our veganism. Sure, there are aspects about veganism that are about humans, but it is not *all* about humans. We are not the ones losing our lives.

The third is in relation to questions or discussion relating to welfare standards—the so-called humane treatment, or organic, happy, cuddly, dreamy exploitation. Any of these topics boil down to one issue: whether we have any good reason to *use* animals in the first place.

Ultimately, keeping the animals as the focus of our vegan advocacy is the critical point. Imagine a wheel, where the animals are the hub and all the other issues are the spokes. The spokes emanate from the hub. However, each element is simultaneously individual and interconnected.

Once we have identified the issues, keep the conversation simple, short and straightforward. We may have occasion to go deeper into the issues even within the same interaction. Often, however, we only have a small window of someone's attention and we should capitalise on that moment. Being educated on the issues is of paramount importance because it will give us the confidence to handle any situation. When we discuss issues that we fully understand, our voices become a very powerful tool because we are able to deliver the message in our own simple and authentic manner. We may not convince people all the time, but at the very least, we will plant the best and strongest seeds possible.

You can go vegan today.

## *Video Advocacy*
**Ben MacEllen, Australia:**

We live in an age where we sometimes feel disconnected from people, but thanks to things like our smartphones, tablets, laptops and personal computers, we can actually reach more people from across the globe using these devices, via recorded video, and video live stream.

Perhaps you don't have time to table or to have one-on-one conversations, but you can grab two minutes here or five minutes there to record a video, and this method of advocacy can be just as effective.

Now, there are as many things that you can do in your video advocacy as there are ways of advocating veganism, from using songs and poetry, to making a vegan recipe, and even presenting a "Thought for the Day." It's a great opportunity to get in touch with and inspire both the nonvegans and other vegans in your life, just by grabbing a few minutes in your day to do wonderful grassroots vegan advocacy.

There are countless apps and programmes you can use to either record video or video live stream, including YouTube and Facebook Live. So whether you're a tech wiz or just your average device user, there's a programme for you.

You might draw your inspiration from books like *Eat Like You Care*, news articles, posts shared on social media, topics about which you feel passionate, that educate, entertain, and even engage people in discussion.

All you need is the determination, enthusiasm and a few minutes to share the Abolitionist message that veganism is the moral baseline.

Lights! Camera! ACTION!

## *The Importance of Questions*
**Frances McCormack, Ireland:**

The importance of the use of questions cannot be underestimated in advocacy: from building rapport to creating broad areas of agreement, questions help your interlocutor feel that they are guiding the conversation and they provide scaffolding that influences your interlocutor to engage in what I term "self-advocacy", responding to your questions in such a way that they convince themselves of the ethical principles that demand veganism.

Elevator pitches, while useful for the new advocate who may feel more confident having prepared responses, can seem stilted, and they put us in the position of defending our veganism. Instead of giving people the opportunity to ask why you're vegan, then, ask why they are not; this will help convey the idea that it is animal exploitation, and not ideas of peace and justice, that needs to be questioned.

Asking questions of your interlocutor can also help disrupt their accepted thinking about animals by causing them to reflect on how they use animals and why; you can even bring them back in time to when they first found out that they were eating animals and how they responded, thus reminding them that they didn't always accept the practice.

Here are some of the kinds of questions you can ask:

Tag questions can build rapport and create agreement: "dogs are so friendly, aren't they?"; "your cat is very affectionate, isn't she?"

Open questions about animals can elicit moral concern. Asking about companion animals is particularly useful in this regard; allow the interlocutor to respond at length, and guide them to think about what sets that animal apart from others in terms of behaviour, preferences, interests, etc. This will help reinforce the idea that animals are persons.

Closed questions can establish shared moral concern: "do you think it's wrong to inflict unnecessary suffering on animals?" These can establish a firm ethical foundation on which you can build to convince your interlocutor of the moral imperative.

Expansive questions can explore any possible objections. They can help your interlocutor clarify a position ("can you give me an example?"), to investigate assumptions and viewpoints ("why do you think that?"), to consider rationale ("are these objections good enough to continue using animals?"; "What do you think causes us to…?"). Such questions help to uncover potential objections that may then be addressed.

Recap questions will help to clear up any points from the discussion that may still stand in the way of your interlocutor becoming vegan ("was there anything we discussed about which you are still uncertain?")

Using questioning requires that we listen attentively to our interlocutor and that we continuously reflect and adapt throughout the conversation. It necessitates that we be patient, but it can reap great rewards in forcing our interlocutor to deconstruct all prior assumptions about animal use.

### *Tabling: How to Get Set Up*
**Damon McDonald, Australia:**

Tabling can be a particularly effective and versatile means of educating people about veganism. People respond to being able to speak with someone in person and have their questions answered and discussed on the spot.

Once you identify where you are going to table, that will dictate your type of set up. I highly recommend putting yourself in a high traffic flow area.

I believe that an impact sign is important. If you want people to approach you to have engaged conversations about veganism, then I believe you must use the word vegan in your main sign.

As far as materials are concerned, I don't believe you need a lot to start off with. Handouts are great for people to take away but they have to be the right handouts that send people to the right places for information. I find the really important thing with tabling though is not the materials but the conversations. The materials may help spark conversations and the signage may bring people in, but it's what we say and how we interact that determines the effectiveness of our advocacy in educating people.

If you're in a regular spot people will come back to you to continue the conversation. Get all set up, but the main aspect of your set up will be and should be educating yourself first. At least, make sure you've read the books *Eat Like You Care* and *The Abolitionist Approach to Animal Rights*. Use the other resources available (such as the Abolitionist Approach website) to really understand what veganism as a moral imperative actually means and how we must convey this to people.

It's also very important that we listen to people, let them speak, ask them questions, really engage them but also try and keep them focused on their own individual moral responsibility to nonhumans. Always focus on bringing the conversation back to the moral message. The more conversations you have, the better you'll get.

If you can start advocating in any way, advocate from an Abolitionist educational perspective--it works—and start now! The nonhumans for whom we're doing this need us to stand up and do everything we can to help and educate people to go vegan and truly shift the paradigm. Only a clear, consistent and uncompromising message of justice will achieve this.

## *Be Prepared to Advocate at All Times*
**Anita Moos, India:**

Advocacy requires self-preparation. While we may be certain of our ethical position, our ability to convince others is a very important component of effective advocacy.

The person to whom we choose to advocate may have preconceived ideas that are initially obstacles to their adopting veganism. Therefore, we must be very clear about what we will say.

Assuming you have found an opening and have steered the conversation in the right direction, you must now have answers that will help ease the worries some people may experience, such as those surrounding food, health, and expense. A good idea is to provide a link to www.howdoigovegan.com that provides mentoring and other helpful information.

At all times, we must stress that veganism is a moral imperative and, as such, its adoption as a moral principle cannot be based on the ease with which one can source "substitute" vegan products. The idea that there must always be available vegan analogues of every animal product is harmful:

It perpetuates the idea that animals are resources. We must be clear that our natural sources of food are plants and not sentient beings.

"Substitute" vegan foods, such as mock meat, while they do assist transitions, are often not healthy as they have high levels of sodium and fat. They also increase the cost of a diet that is otherwise very affordable.

To be confident while advocating, we must know what we are talking about. The best way of doing this is to educate ourselves by reading. Online reading groups like the IVA [internationalvegan.org] can assist in this regard. Our confidence in our advocacy goes a long way towards convincing others.

If you have presented your arguments and answered many questions, but are presented with a question that you cannot answer, offer to find out and get back to the person. Handing out contact information is a great idea anyway because you must follow up with people to whom you have advocated. Doing so will also demonstrate your conviction and willingness to help.

If you experience frustration, remember that you are doing this for the animals. You are their voice and you must sound logical, composed and ready to help.

People may want to talk about the environmental or health consequences of being vegan. It can be tempting to promote these reasons. But remember that while people may go "vegan" temporarily because of such reasons, those who stay vegan do it for ethical reasons and understand that veganism is a matter of social justice and animal rights. Veganism is the moral baseline and that is what we must always say.

We all advocate with our own unique set of circumstances, and our advocacy therefore takes on many different forms. Our knowledge, willingness to educate, and level of preparation, though, must remain constant. When we are prepared, preparing others becomes easy. So let's all educate ourselves and go out there to advocate and welcome others into our wonderful vegan world.

### *Advocating to a Silent Audience Online*
### Alan O'Reilly, Ireland:

When we are engaged in conversations on social media sites, such as Facebook, there will nearly always be an unseen audience of people who are not participating but can nevertheless be influenced by what is said. We need to be mindful of those sometimes affectionately called "the lurkers" when we advocate. Here are a few tips to ensure that we represent vegans and veganism favourably on social media at all times:

Present your comments firmly but politely, even when faced with others who are aggressive and offensive. When watching an exchange between one party who is civil and another who is obnoxious, the uncommitted will automatically favour the former, regardless of content.

Maintain control of the conversation. Stick to the topic(s) being discussed and avoid being led into a derailed argument. Point out straw men and other logical fallacies and refuse to engage them. (For a discussion of logical fallacies, please see Appendix 2.)

Answer every question as though it is the first time you have been asked it. There may be someone out there who doesn't know we can get protein from plants or that plants don't have feelings too!

Present as much information as possible. Give links to sources that onlookers can research for themselves.

Know when to bow out of a conversation that has become circular or otherwise counterproductive. Do not try to "win" arguments or have the last word.

Remember that we are advocating on behalf of the victims of injustice. Our advocacy should present information that enables people to understand why they should be vegan and helps them to become vegan. We sow seeds in fertile soil, often for others to nurture at a later date: ground that we cannot see but which certainly exists on social media sites.

## Vegan Educational Broadcasting
### Jeff Perz, Australia:

One method of creative, nonviolent vegan education is hosting a podcast/vodcast/FM-radio-show. The focus of the show could be on human rights and the environment, with progressive politics, and it would include a discussion of Abolitionist veganism.

The organizer of the *World Vegan Summit*, Bob Linden, has, for many years, produced and hosted the excellent radio program, *Go Vegan Radio*. That program has been an important part of the vegan movement. But my thought here involves a different format.

The idea is to avoid having an explicitly vegan show, for the purpose of attracting as many nonvegans in the audience as possible. If the show had four segments, there would always be one segment that clearly and persuasively argues for ethical veganism from the Abolitionist Approach. The placement of the vegan segment could vary from show to show.

A broadcast like this would start out small and hopefully attract a larger audience over time. Local community radio stations are often happy for people to get broadcasting training and start new shows. Those same FM radio shows can serve as podcasts and vodcasts.

One type of radio show is an indie news broadcast, with an Abolitionist vegan editorial. As the show develops, it could have interviews, or live advocacy discussions between nonvegans and vegan educators.

If you did your own broadcast, you could make it into anything that you are passionate about. As long as you are vegan, educate yourself about the Abolitionist Approach and the purpose of your show is to make new vegans, then this method of activism can be a powerful tool. The goal is to reach as many progressively minded nonvegans as possible.

### *The Moral Predicate*
### Christian Sanchez, United States:

Becoming a vegan is not some extreme or far-fetched idea. In fact, veganism is an idea with which most of us already agree. That is, most of us already accept the predicate to becoming a vegan. The question to always ask is: "Do you believe it's wrong to unnecessarily inflict suffering and death on animals?" I ask this question in almost all of my interactions with nonvegans. Most people agree that it is wrong to unnecessarily inflict suffering and death on nonhuman persons, yet they aren't vegan yet.

After the nonvegan answers your question, it's important to follow up and inform them that 99.999% of all of the ways in which we inflict suffering and death on animals is *completely* unnecessary because we can live happy and healthy lives without using animals. We do not need to use animals in order to live.

By asking this morally intuitive question and following up, we are helping nonvegans bridge the gap in their minds between what they truly believe is the morally right thing to do and where they are at now morally.

Ask the morally intuitive question at any point in your advocacy conversation. Use it as an opener and you'll save yourself the trouble of discussing irrelevant topics that have nothing to do with morality! The sooner you use the question, the sooner you'll direct the conversation and lead it home.

And we do.

## When Health is the Issue
### Bill Tara, Ireland and Scotland:

Let's face it, most humans are self-centered. That's not to say that they are bad, simply limited in their range of concern. It is part of my job, and joy, to help them widen their perspectives.

The issue of animals as the default setting as a food source has been driven deep in the modern psyche. Many people think that milk and flesh are essential for human health; it is a mythology that is stubborn in its resolve. Several paths open up for us to reverse this idea.

There is now ample evidence that our food choices harm individuals, society and the environment as well as finding their basis in the unneeded suffering and murder of animals. The case is no longer a fringe belief – it is a provable and undeniable fact. Only the childish ridicule of those who resist any social change is closed to the conversation.

That regard can best be addressed by advocates being well informed and following a diet that ensures maximum potential for health. A healthy diet is not simply marked by what we don't eat, but what we do eat.

The emphasis on whole unprocessed foods, local foods, seasonal foods, grains, beans, vegetables, fruit and nuts define the first steps down that path. This way of eating defines the best route for the health and vitality that people expect from dietary change. It may not be the final goal but it is always a step in the right direction.

## Advocating for Veganism: Taking Advantage of the Unexpected Opportunities
### Peggy Warren, United States:

With just a little preparation, it's easy to be ready to take advantage of an Every Day Opportunity (EDO). This is something everyone can and should do. So how does this work?

The three key elements are: be prepared; look for opportunities; act.

The first step in being prepared is to have advocacy materials ready and available. I always keep business-sized www.howdoigovegan.com cards and Abolitionist Approach pamphlets on me. These can be printed at home or professionally. You need to be positive. Believe that people *want* to learn about veganism. Keep this in mind when you approach them, and don't be afraid to smile.

- Next, look for opportunities when you:
- Work, jog, walk, socialize or play;
- Bank, shop, get gas;
- Talk with sales or customer service people;
- Use public transportation;
- Eat out;
- Visit the food bank, etc.

Soon you discover that EDOs can pop up anywhere, anytime. Be ready for them.

Third, the most important thing to do once you see an opening is to *act*. If you hear the words, "Is there anything else I can do for you?" say "Yes, I would like you to go vegan," and offer printed resources. If you hear someone speaking about how much they love their nonhuman companion, acknowledge that and ask if they have considered going vegan.

Mention that if we care about animals, the least we can do is not eat, wear or use them, and that there is no difference between the animals we love and those we eat. Whatever you say, always provide resources for people to learn more about how and why we all need to be vegan.

Without notice you could find yourself faced with an advocacy opportunity. So be prepared, look for opportunities, then act. If you can only hand someone a flyer or a card, please *do so*. Nonhumans not only need our voice, we *owe* it to them.

### *Health and Vegan Advocacy*
**Marlene Watson-Tara, Ireland and Scotland:**

My mission and vision to create a healthy world for all of the species we share this planet with has been going strong for more than forty years. Healthy people create a healthy world.; sick people create a sick world.

Being vegan is not a diet; it is a way of looking at the world as a whole that has a profound effect not only on who we are as individuals but on everything and everyone we encounter.

Clients always say to me, "Marlene, since I changed my life and embraced veganism, it's like I have had a veil lifted from my eyes. I see differently, I feel differently, I am different." Why do they feel this shift in consciousness? Because they are living without causing pain or suffering to any other beings. They connect the dots. We are all one.

My advocacy therefore comes from being a food activist and teaching the masses how we can all create good health in mind, body, and spirit by what we choose to have at the end of our fork daily. When *you* are a healthy human, your heart will be so full and open to helping to guide and change others towards veganism. As the wonderful Nelson Mandela said, "Education is the most powerful weapon which you can use to change the world."

I teach my wee rhyme which has made its way to 25 countries via our students who graduate on our Macrobiotic Health Coach Course. I will continue to switch on more "lighthouses" around the planet as long as I breathe. So please join me in repeating:

*Food makes the blood,*
*Blood makes the cells,*
*Cells make the tissue,*
*Tissue makes the organs,*
*And here we be.*

## There Is Something for Everyone to Do!

Everyone has their own talents and interests, and everyone can adapt those talents to Abolitionist advocacy.

In Chapter 2, we talked about the importance of internet advocacy. There are many essays on animal ethics posted every day on the internet. Most of these essays reflect the dominant welfarist paradigm but have comment sections that allow Abolitionists to raise and to discuss the Abolitionist perspective and to engage readers on the moral and practical problems with the welfarist approach. In addition to the Abolitionists in this chapter, others, such as Balint Balasa, Linda McKenzie (www.voxvegan.com), and Carter Felder, participate in discussions on these sites and do an excellent job in educating people about the Abolitionist Approach. Carter and Jeffrey Coolwater manage a number of Abolitionist sites on Twitter and Instagram

Educating people about how to remove animal products from their diet is also very important. Abolitionists like Frances McCormack and Marlene Watson-Tara, who have contributions in this chapter, have done a spectacular job in developing cheap and easy vegan recipes. Abolitionist Vincent Guihan has written *New American Vegan* (https://goo.gl/Ddj1RP), which has a range of recipes from more easy to those for the dedicated vegan chef.

Those who teach in universities, colleges, and other academic settings have a marvelous opportunity to educate students. And scholarship that seeks to shift the paradigm away from welfarism and the property status of animals, and toward Abolition and the personhood of nonhuman animals, is yet another form of activism. In addition to the work we have done (www.abolitionistapproach.com/books), we note the work of Professor Gary Steiner (www.facstaff.bucknell.edu/gsteiner), who has written excellent scholarship in the Abolitionist tradition.

Everyone who embraces the Abolitionist philosophy can make a unique contribution. It's just a matter of deciding to commit to Abolitionist advocacy.

\*\*\*\*\*\*\*\*\*

In the next chapter, we will consider Abolitionist vegan advocacy in a very challenging context: where there is economic deprivation.

# Chapter 4

## Advocacy in Low-Income Communities

The animal rights movement has not served low-income communities well. Because low-income communities, particularly urban communities, have a higher proportion of people of color, the movement must also be said not to have served people of color well.

The grassroots approach of Abolitionist veganism is particularly suited for outreach in poorer communities. It does not require a significant outlay of money or the backing of an organization; it only requires people talking to people and some follow-up.

A preliminary comment: we maintain and repeat that the transition to Abolitionist veganism is easy for the vast majority of people. We also maintain that the transition can be made consistently by people in low-income communities. But we are aware of the specific challenges faced by low-income communities because we spend a lot of time in those communities. Everything—raising children, finding work, travel, education, personal safety—is more difficult if you are poor. Everything is more difficult if you have a disability. Everything is more difficult if you do not feel safe in your living surroundings. In that way, the transition to veganism, which is easy for the vast majority of people, may pose specific challenges to those who are in difficult social circumstances.

But we are *not* talking about people who cannot commit to Abolitionist veganism because of where they are on some spiritual or psychological "journey": we are talking about where they are physically and socially located.

We will focus on "food deserts" in the United States, where people do not have regular or convenient access to affordable, nutritious food, but similar problems may be found in many areas of the world, each with its local causes and challenges. Definitions of a food desert vary, but the U.S. government estimates that 23.5 million people, including 6.5 million children, confront food access problems, as they live an inconvenient distance from a supermarket and often do not have a car. Half of these people, a disproportionate number, are people of color. Moreover, some 2.3 million people live in low-income rural areas that are more than 10 miles from a grocery store. Limited public transportation in rural areas makes food access particularly difficult. Without convenient access to affordable, healthy food, many residents in cities rely on fast-food outlets. People living in the poorest areas of the U.S. have 2.5 times the exposure to fast-food restaurants as those in the wealthiest areas.

Food deserts pose at least two problems—access and cost—that will affect residents differently depending on their other circumstances. When we first became vegan, we lived in two of the biggest cities in the U.S. at a time when the densest urban areas were not well served by supermarkets. For several of those years, we did not have a car. Finding a range of vegan food took thought and planning. But young, urban professionals who need to find access to vegan food are very differently situated than are poor, elderly, or physically challenged residents who do not have transportation or resources to easily travel to a well-stocked supermarket. If you face a long bus ride to a supermarket, you may rely on convenience stores or the local bodega, which likely offers a limited range of food products and this can make healthy, and healthy vegan, eating more difficult. Lack of food access correlates with both high rates of obesity and incidence of diabetes and poses a serious problem for the health of children.

Food deserts present a particular barrier for people in poor communities who are considering becoming vegan. Residents of poor communities are already very concerned to provide healthy food for their families and vegan advocates can assist in ensuring that they have the information necessary to change to a vegan diet. No one fights harder to feed their children than parents in poverty. The idea that poor people do not care about healthy eating is a stereotype that needs to be ditched as quickly as that of Ronald Reagan's "welfare queen."

Mainstream vegan organizations have largely ignored poor communities: the very communities who may need assistance in adopting veganism and who would reap the most benefit from a healthy vegan diet. In this chapter, we will explore two questions. We will first explore why this happened. Why has the mainstream "animal movement" done such a poor job on outreach and support to poor communities? We will then examine what can be done to remedy the problem.

## Why Has the "Animal Movement" Failed Low-Income Communities?

The answer is surely multi-faceted, but two reasons are clear and apparent.

*First*, the mainstream "animal movement," which consists of the large, corporate charities, does not promote veganism as a general matter to *any* community, much less the poor communities. The large groups promote welfare reform: they promote larger cages and supposedly more "humane" torture. They promote single-issue campaigns focused on fur, the killing of whales, the eating of dogs, and the use of wild animals in circuses. To the extent that these groups promote veganism at all, they promote it as one way of reducing suffering, along with cage-free eggs and crate-free pork. So the animal movement has not reached out to poor communities with a clear vegan message because the animal movement hasn't reached out to *any* community to promote a clear vegan message. On the contrary, the "mainstream" explicitly rejects the idea that veganism is a moral imperative.

*Second*, the large corporate groups do not target poor communities in any event. Corporate charities, which use professional fundraisers, know who they are targeting, and they are not going to pay to do mass mailing solicitations in the poorer zip codes. Is this because those in poor areas don't contribute to charities? No. On the contrary, persons who have lower incomes tend to give a *higher* percentage of their income to charitable endeavors including churches than those in higher income brackets. But people in poor communities may be less likely to respond to the sorts of campaigns that these corporate animal charities promote. They may be less concerned about who is the "sexiest" vegetarian/ vegan of the year, or whether the Chinese are eating dogs.

We have been teaching in a low-income urban area—Newark, New Jersey—for decades. Many of our students come from that community. Many times we have had students ask us why animal people are concerned about what's going on in China when there are slaughterhouses that are killing cows, sheep, and chickens all throughout the New York/New Jersey area. We have no better answer for them than that these groups find it easier to get donations from people who are eating other animals by demonizing people in Asia who eat dogs.

The main group targeted by large animal charities is the group that identifies as part of the "animal movement." These are, for the most part, middle class people, most of whom are not vegan, who have some sort of concern about animals and who are more than happy to give a donation so that they can be told that they are a part of the "movement" at the same time they continue eat, wear, or use animals. They are perfectly happy with being told that they are not capable of making a difference as individuals by going vegan and encouraging others to do so, and that they should just send their donation to support the "real" professionals do whatever single-issue horror-story campaign is most effective at tugging at the heartstrings and opening the wallets.

This donor group is very receptive to exactly what these large charities promote: more "humane" treatment; single-issue campaigns aimed at fur, the Chinese, and circuses; and reducetarianism. To the extent that these charities promote veganism, it is usually in the form of high-priced processed meat or dairy substitutes, or expensive clothing from famous designers. These are not the sorts of campaigns that resonate within low-income communities.

Interestingly, but perhaps in the end, not surprisingly, we have found that when grassroots advocates engage, one to one, in a discussion about the change to Abolitionist veganism as a way of life, it resonates and has more appeal in disadvantaged communities.

## How Can Abolitionist Vegans Advocate in Low-Income Communities?

If we agree that veganism must be the moral baseline, and that it makes no sense to try to address any specific instance of animal treatment until we challenge the institutions of animal use within the framework of Abolitionist veganism, how can advocates be effective in discussing veganism in disadvantaged communities?

We are up against the multifaceted problem of social inequality, which is not only financial, but also reflects that the poor have less of a political voice. But an ethical principle can resonate in many diverse communities. We often hear the accusation that food insecurity and the lack of access may make veganism impracticable in poorer communities, and that, because there is a higher concentration of people of color in poor urban neighborhoods, insisting that veganism is a moral imperative is racist. We reject that position. To suggest that poor people, including people of color, are not receptive to veganism, or find it too difficult, is insulting to those people, and diminishes the frankly heroic way in which people with few advantages live their lives in ways that should make those with more advantages ashamed. So if we are going to advocate for something, let's be serious about literally bringing it forth. Moreover, the recognition that our use of animals poses ethical problems is well-recognized in low-income communities, where many lively discussions are already going on. Whether from the Rastafarian or Buddhist traditions, or in modern music and poetry, there is already focus on the animal issue.

Poverty contaminates *everything*. Everything is more difficult when you are economically disadvantaged, economically stressed, economically insecure. But what progress has been made in any area has often come as the result of herculean efforts on behalf of a principle. The Montgomery Bus Boycott that brought Dr. Martin Luther King to the national stage in the United States is a good example. What was to be a one-day boycott continued for over a year. It required steadfast determination and caused hardship. Don't believe that poor and disadvantaged people will not act consistently on their principles. That is both unfair and factually wrong.

Abolitionist vegan advocacy is a grassroots activity. It involves doing something very different from what the corporate charities are doing. It does not involve asking for donations. It does involve helping with education and with practical ideas about implementation. Abolitionists are not targeting their audience based on what they can get from that audience, but rather, what they can offer that audience. Abolitionists should never be discouraged by the accusation that somehow this is "missionary work" that should be criticized or even condemned. We Abolitionists should—and must—talk to everyone we can, wherever we can. It is bizarre that anyone would criticize the past history of animal charities not reaching out to poorer communities, but then criticize individual advocates who reach out to other communities.

If you live in a poor community, you will be ideally placed to assist others in navigating through the practical challenges that must be addressed. If you can do it, other people will see that they can do it also. If you yourself do not presently live in a poor community, make inquiries to see if you can hook up with a present resident so that you can work together. Local advocates will benefit from an ally who can assist their team and also may be able to make the logistics easier, by providing transportation, materials, food samples, and supplies.

We would suggest that anyone doing vegan advocacy and vegan support in poorer areas, whether or not they are resident in that area, should keep in mind several things.

*First,* be respectful of the experiences of those you are meeting. Their lives and their history may be very different from your own. You will only find out how you can help if you ask. Ask how you can help in practical ways: ask what information would be helpful. Ask if you can provide the benefit of your resources, your learning, the fact that you have helped others before. *Adopt an attitude of service.* There will be organizations and structures of community already at work—find out how you can assist within that framework. Teachers, clergy, social workers, and grandparents have a knowledge and perspective that is invaluable.

As we emphasized in Chapter 1, we think that advocacy should not be a matter of showing off and using all sorts of jargon. The best ideas are simple. They can be communicated in simple, plain language. Wherever you are advocating, but perhaps most importantly in poor communities that are at an educational disadvantage, or where you may not share a first language with your listener, when you are introducing new ideas, present those ideas clearly. Let's not clog the message with all the "isms" and "ologies" and heavy, stacked sentences. That's so tedious in every situation! Don't make your listener do a running translation of what you are saying as if they were reading a MRI report. You are not insulting your listener by speaking in plain language, in fact, just the opposite. If you are on the street talking about epistemologies, "liberatory praxis" (in fact, for good measure, any sort of "praxis") and "critical" this, that and the other, clear your throat, take a deep breath and start again. That stuff gets in articles that thirty people will read, and into too many student papers. It says "hey, look at me, the smart one!" It does not *communicate*, and in many situations, it is insulting.

*Second*, educate yourself!

At first, veganism may seem to require a considerable change that is overwhelming or too burdensome for people who already have a lot of social and economic problems on their plate. People will only engage with you on the possibility of veganism if it seems possible given their situation. Advocates need to be ready with ideas and encouragement, both on the practical problems that poor communities may face, and some ready solutions that can ease the necessary adjustments.

Let's think of some of the main areas where poorer communities could use some help in going vegan.

*1. Healthy vegan food need not be expensive, and is usually cheaper.*

Many people are worried that a vegan diet is expensive. The large, corporate charities, which    rarely advocate for veganism themselves, have done a great job of presenting a vegan diet as difficult and expensive, so grassroots Abolitionist vegan advocates need to quickly counter that perception. Have some ideas and facts at your fingertips to reassure that vegan food is not expensive. Wholesome, plant-based, appetizing food is usually considerably cheaper than animal products. Such foods are featured on www.howdoigovegan.com, which very deliberately showcases inexpensive meals that are easily prepared from common ingredients. Take cards with that website address, or flyers featuring a dish that a family could prepare that very evening when you table in poorer communities. Ensure that your message is as practical as what is next put on the dinner table. Reassure your listener that they do not have to turn to the processed imitation animal products that are indeed expensive—and not particularly nutritious. Reassure them that while organic, out-of-season vegetables and fruits are expensive, it is not necessary to purchase those foods in order to plan their new vegan meals.

*2. How can we improve access to vegan food?*

So many problems are made easier with a little extra money—veganism included. Learn some basic facts about what assistance is available to poorer communities for food security.

An obvious area for study is becoming familiar with the government benefit programs in your area. In the United States, become familiar with the SNAP program. That's the Supplemental Nutrition Assistance Program—which most people refer to as "Food Stamps." There are 43 million recipients of SNAP benefits, but millions more are eligible and not receiving those benefits. About 25% of eligible people do not receive their benefit. So, go to the USDA website and familiarize yourself with the eligibility rules and the application process.

Newark, New Jersey, where we have worked for many years, is a very poor city with very high rates of every sort of crime. A lot of the buildings that were burned out during the civil rights clashes of the 1960s are still there—empty shells, weed-choked, crumbling. They tell every child who walks past on the way to school "We don't care about you." But we are pleased that so many in the university community are active on issues of civil rights, environmental racism (because every toxic substance you can imagine from DDT to Agent Orange has been manufactured in the Newark area), and poverty issues. The law clinics at Rutgers represent many local people before government agencies to ensure that they receive the benefits to which they are entitled—whether education, all aspects of health including mental health, housing, or SNAP benefits. We also help people to fill out forms or find the addresses of agencies they need to contact. If our students can learn that material, so can you.

If a person has a language barrier, or poor literacy, getting a letter about their benefits can be confusing and frightening. Everyone reading this book can help in that situation. People with special skills and perspectives, such as teachers, social workers, nurses, community organizers or clergy can be particularly helpful, but everyone can offer assistance. Abolitionist vegans can also develop an expertise to assist in providing vegan food after natural disasters, or to prisoners, or to home-bound elderly or disabled persons.

SNAP benefits do not provide a large amount of money, and as that money has to stretch a long way, getting an adequate diet can be challenging. Remember, this is a problem for *every* person—whether vegan or not—trying to provide nutritious meals for a family on a very limited income. For this reason, much of the food on the website www.howdoigovegan.com is specifically targeted at low-cost meals that can be simply planned. Emphasize that nutritional requirements can be met more cheaply by a vegan diet than an animal-based diet.

But we still have the problem of geographic access to food. Our traditional business model for providing groceries is one cause of food deserts. Food deserts in the US are largely a result of the "white flight" of the 1950s and 1960s. When middle class, predominately white, residents fled the inner city, a lot of tax dollars went with them. Mortgage companies used "redlining" to carve out areas where they did not want to lend money, stopping investment in those areas, and business closed and left: so went the grocery stores. The result is that communities including all races face food insecurity in low-income areas.

Today, many groups, and even the federal government itself, are looking to bring healthy food back to these areas, but a problem long in the making will not bow to a swift solution. For example, in Newark, a new supermarket opened with great fanfare in the heart of the city in 2013. The Mayor praised its arrival as another step in the revitalization of the city. A year later, the store closed. Construction delays contributed to a rocky start, but the real problem turned out to be that the store had not secured its license to accept food stamp payments from the Women, Infants and Children (WIC) program and 15% of its business would have come from those payments. We're going to need business initiatives that take into consideration the real problems that exist. If it was simple, it would have been fixed long ago.

There are two ways to solve the problem of geographic access: encourage or enable existing vendors to add produce or bring in new produce vendors under a new model. It is important to know how the poorer communities that you may be working in can benefit from the increased access to fresh fruits and vegetables and a wider range of food options.

Let's celebrate the farmers' markets! They are springing up all over the place in locations where you might not expect to see them, and they can make a world of difference to a new vegan. Don't know where your local farmers are bringing their wares? Here's the website for farmers' markets located throughout the United States: https://goo.gl/f9osfp, and here is the National Farmers Market Directory, with location, directions, operating times, product offerings, and forms of payment accepted: https://goo.gl/oV6tD1.

Wherever you are in the United States, put in your zip code. Tell everyone about those great resources and support them yourself. The days of choosing a wizened iceberg lettuce at the corner store, and finding no fresh fruits apart from bananas are over. Keep the demand for easy access to nutritious vegan food growing, and also encourage your local community to make those markets better, by extending the months of the year they can operate if provided with sheltered selling space in winter for example, or by ensuring that customers receiving government benefits can make their purchases there.

Many government programs in the United States, and probably in other countries where you may be advocating, provide funds for nutrition assistance with a card or token to ensure that the funds are used for approved purchases. The Farmers Market Nutrition Program provides coupons to low-income mothers and seniors that can be redeemed at markets. Green markets can accept a SNAP debit card using the government's Electronic Benefit Transfer (E.B.T.) system. A wireless point of sale terminal can be obtained free of charge by the vendor. This makes farmers' markets more accessible to lower income customers, with the added benefit for vegans that families receive a $2 coupon for every $5 in E.B.T. sales at a farmers' market—a 40% increase in their purchasing power. It also helps local vendors, who report a nearly 40% increase in monthly food stamp sales when they have the terminals to accept E.B.T. transactions.

While we can surely blame the government for not remedying the conditions of poverty and its close ally, structural racism, there are now finally government programs that can make veganism a little easier despite the macro conditions in food deserts. The USDA has an articulated policy of making fresh fruits and vegetables more accessible to those on SNAP benefits and is implanting that policy. There is a push to encourage farmers markets in urban areas, and the program we just highlighted, whereby if SNAP benefits are used to purchase fruits and vegetables, the recipient receives an additional 40% to spend, is a significant boon in a household budget. That's good news for those choosing veganism: not only are the foods they choose cheaper than their previous animal product purchases, but they also receive a bonus of 40% *more* spending power. And veganism is too expensive, we heard?

There are programs to get more fresh food and vegetables into preschools, into all levels of grade education, into the hands of carers, and sent to Native American communities, who have been shamefully underserved on every front, with grave health and social outcomes. This is a start—late and too little but a start—and vegan educators need to know what foods are available in their communities, all the while pushing to resolve these serious social issues.

Clearly, food insecurity is a pervasive problem but vegan advocates can offer assistance and encouragement to new vegans as they navigate through the changing system of food provision. Apart from your one-on-one Abolitionist vegan advocacy, it is important to be aware of existing and proposed community and legislative initiatives to improve the situation. There are organizations and individuals who will be able to educate you about the work that they have been doing and how you can learn from their experience and example, and the social justice campaigns where you can lend a hand. There are creative initiatives on the national, and local levels, even down to community organizing and city-block initiatives, that bring fresh fruits and vegetables and other healthy vegan food products into poorly served areas.

As we mentioned above, access problems can be addressed in two ways: finding new outlets for fresh food delivery, or by increasing the fresh offerings in existing outlets. In New York City, there are now over 50 greenmarkets, and the Green Cart initiative, whereby grants are offered to small businesses to cover the start-up cost (around $1800) to operate carts selling fresh fruits and vegetables, has had great success in providing reliable delivery of fresh produce at a reasonable price, in addition to providing employment and self-sufficiency to local workers, many of whom are recent immigrants. The initiative offers 1000 new permits for street vendors who can sell only raw fruits and vegetables in areas underserved by traditional supermarkets where there has been very limited access to such produce. The model of this initiative, which has been a successful partnership between philanthropic organizations and the city government, has led to similar initiatives in other cities including Washington, D.C. and Philadelphia.

The second approach—getting more fresh offerings in local existing outlets—has led to initiatives such as New York's Healthy Bodegas Initiative (https://goo.gl/pkntEq). Bodegas that stock a wider range of healthy foods can receive assistance such as business and marketing advice, and also importantly, grants for the installation of refrigerators and shelving. Similarly, in Philadelphia, The Food Trust, which has been tackling food deserts by various approaches, has started the Healthy Corner Store Initiative (https://goo.gl/N9ZoB7).

The lack of refrigeration has been one of the main reasons that local bodegas and convenience stores have not purchased stock of healthy, fresh food, as the perish rate made them unprofitable and impractical. Other similar programs across the country have been noted by the National Institutes of Health to significantly improve the range of diet choices in underserved neighborhoods, offering positive health outcomes and outlook. There are also some happy vegans!

To make such initiatives work, we will need business people who are willing to pursue innovative approaches where traditional models have failed, and thoughtful government subsidies to make the economics work.

And we must not forget that many people are subject to the degree of food insecurity that leads them to rely on food banks, community kitchens, and places where excess food that has been collected is distributed.

In New York, City Harvest has a long record of getting food that would otherwise be wasted into the hands of people whose food budgets cannot stretch to the end of the month. In Philadelphia, Philabundance does similar gathering and distribution and has been remarkably creative in reaching areas where food is most needed. The food needs to go where the hunger and food insecurity is worst. Philabundance sets up travelling farmers' markets where the produce is free to visitors without means testing and without affecting any other benefits they may receive. The distributions are at the same nine locations in Pennsylvania and New Jersey at the same time each week, those times and locations being posted on their website. Locations include churches and community centers, but Philabundance has also even set up distribution stands at busy intersections, and under a major road underpass. *1.6 million pounds* of fresh, free produce got into the hands of underserved residents by these innovative approaches in 2016.

Philabundance has recently challenged the traditional business model of supermarket distribution by opening its first nonprofit supermarket in Chester, Pennsylvania, a poor community. Chester had not had a grocery store since 2001 and 54% of its residents polled responded that they had to travel too far for groceries. Twenty-four percent of Chester's residents considered themselves very food insecure, compared to approximately 4% statewide. The new store is open for twelve hours a day, seven days a week so that shift workers and working parents have convenient access. SNAP benefits are accepted. Additional similar stores are planned.

And to give a new and somewhat Biblical twist, Philabundance volunteers coordinate with local farmers to "glean" in the fields after crops are harvested—picking up produce that would otherwise simply be ploughed into the earth. How effective is that? Philabundance got 220,000 pounds of gleaned fresh produce into the hands of hungry families in 2016. That was someone's bright idea—a "why couldn't we…?" moment—that was turned into effective action, and it can be replicated across the country, on large scale or small, by school children, college students, or retired people who want to take practical steps to address real needs. Volunteers can get information from their website about times and locations of gleaning events, and sign up for a shift—

exercise, fresh air and a good cause!

Food insecurity is pervasive, entrenched and challenging, but we must be clear that we are not advocating Abolitionist veganism in areas where it is impossible to respect the fundamental rights of nonhuman animals. Advocates armed with practical advice and solutions, not just theory, can encourage, inform and assist in poor communities.

Know your area, know the programs—fill stomachs as well as hearts when you advocate.

## Some Final Points

We hope that this chapter has given you some ideas about doing Abolitionist vegan advocacy in low-income areas. The information about programs contained herein may change over time but our intention was to provide a framework so that you can think productively about these issues. To the extent that we have discussed particular programs, we have used those that are local to us. We have no affiliation with these organizations and they do not espouse Abolitionist principles. We mention them because they offer some solutions to the problem of access to plant foods. The idea was not so much to focus on those programs but to give you an idea of the sorts of things that may exist in your area. In any event, *wherever* you are, what remains constant is the need for you to educate yourself about similar resources and opportunities of which people of low-income can avail themselves.

Some "animal advocates" claim that those who are poor don't have a moral obligation not to exploit animals. We reject that as just another attempt to reject veganism as a moral imperative. Just as someone who is poor has an obligation not to assault a neighbor to get food, that person has a fundamental obligation not to exploit nonhuman animals. We have never found people in low-income areas to have the slightest problem in understanding this. It is usually middle-class "animal advocates" who tell us that poor people or single mothers simply cannot be expected to understand the concept of veganism as a moral imperative. That is wrong as a matter of morality and it is insulting to those in such communities.

Finally, earlier in the chapter, we mentioned the claim that Abolitionist vegans who advocate in low-income communities are doing "missionary work" that should be condemned. Again, such claims usually come from middle-class "animal advocates" who seem to do little in these communities apart from talking about them. But irrespective of who makes the claim, the claim is wrong and just another attempt to discourage advocacy about veganism as a moral imperative. We have an obligation to talk to anyone and everyone about veganism as a matter of morality and as a matter of health.

\*\*\*\*\*\*\*\*\*

We will now move on to Part Two of the book.

# Part Two: The *What* of Abolitionist Vegan Advocacy

In this second portion, we will address substantive advocacy issues in different contexts—*what* you say when you advocate.

In Chapter 5, we talk about getting people to see that there is no difference between the animals whom they love or care about and those whom they eat or wear.

In Chapter 6, we discuss veganism and the concept of "unnecessary suffering."

In Chapter 7, we focus on veganism and the concept of rights.

In Chapter 8, we discuss how to deal with other animal advocates who reject veganism as a moral baseline.

In Chapter 9, we present some brief notes on dealing with family and friends.

In Chapter 10, we consider how to deal with those who want to go vegan but are anxious about doing so.

In Chapter 11, we discuss how to deal with objections to veganism that you encounter during your advocacy.

In Chapter 12, we consider some ideas about advocating other aspects of the Abolitionist Approach.

# Chapter 5

## Veganism and the Animals You Love or Care About

In order for a person to think of veganism as a reasonable thing to do, it is necessary that they stop seeing nonhuman animals as *things* to eat, wear, or otherwise use. They need to see that animals matter *morally*.

For many people, that is a significant shift in the way they think about animals. The most effective way to persuade them to make that shift is to focus them on situations in which they have already had this recognition and then get them to generalize that recognition.

As soon as someone knows that you are an "animal person," whether or not they know you are a vegan, what are some of the typical things people say to you?

They tell you that they love animals as a general matter.

They tell you about animals with whom they presently have a relationship or had one in the past: you hear about their present and past dogs, cats, gerbils, rabbits, etc. They may even show you pictures! They almost always tell you how much they love their nonhuman friends.

They tell you about something that they've read or heard recently concerning the suffering or killing of animals. For example, they mention the eating of dogs in Asia, or the killing of dolphins in Japan, or the shooting of a lion by a trophy hunter, or the killing of an animal in a zoo in order to protect a child who entered the animal's enclosure. These sorts of stories cause many nonvegans to become outraged.

Whenever we hear one of these three things from people—and believe us, we hear them a great deal—we always respond the same way: we applaud them for their concern; we express our happiness that they "love" animals, that they have or have had wonderful relationships with animals, or that they are outraged about something they have read about or seen on TV or on the internet.

But then, in the *very next breath*, we ask them a simple and straightforward question: *What is the difference between the animals you love or about whom you have concern and the ones you eat, wear, or otherwise treat as things or resources?*

That *always* starts an interesting discussion. The reason it is interesting is that there is *no* good answer to that question. There is no difference that is morally relevant between the animals we eat or otherwise exploit and those we love or about whom we have moral concern. Therefore, this discussion cannot help but lead the person in the direction of recognizing the moral personhood of animals. The challenge is to guide them further in the direction of moral personhood.

Keep in mind what we are trying to do: we are trying to get others to conclude that animals are morally valuable and that they should not, therefore, exploit them. The beauty of this strategy is that it builds on the fact that people have *already* embraced the idea that *some* animals matter morally. You need to get them to generalize their moral concern to *all* animals. But they are your ally in this inquiry in that the two of you share the starting point.

Here are some examples of discussions you might have focusing on this strategy. *You* can have these sorts of exchanges every day: *you* can make a difference.

## Sample Discussion: Veganism in a Vet's Office

We have had *many* discussions about veganism in veterinary offices and they all go more or less the same way. In this particular instance, Anna had taken Katie, our rescued border collie who was then about 19 years old, for a visit. The appointments were running late so she had a few minutes before she and Katie were called in. There was another person sitting in the office with her. The other person was with a golden retriever who appeared to be very old. We had recently lost our rescued golden retriever. What follows is our recollection of the conversation from some notes Anna jotted down later that same day.

Anna: "Your little friend has a lovely face. He reminds me of the retriever we just lost recently. She was 14. Her muzzle became gray in the same pattern as his is."

The other person: "He's 12 now. He's in relatively good shape but his hearing is almost gone and he's getting more lethargic. I know it won't be a very long time and I'm really dreading it."

"Yes, they really are members of the family, aren't they?"

"That's for sure. I've had dogs all my life. Cats as well. I've got two and two now. I'm a real animal lover."

"You know, it's interesting. We have such a confused way of relating to animals."

"What do you mean?"

"Well, we have very meaningful relationships with our dogs and cats and we regard them as individuals whom we really love. But most of us eat animals. And there's no difference between the animals we love and the animals we eat."

"Well yes, but we've got to eat something although I agree that we don't treat animals very well and that's not right."

"No, that's not the case. It's not necessary to eat any animal foods. Neither I nor my partner has had any in more than 30 years now and we're both fine."

"So you're a vegetarian?"

"Actually, we're vegans. We don't eat or wear any animals or go to zoos and things like that."

"I saw all that controversy about Sea World. I'd never go to a place like that. Those poor animals."

"Exactly. Neither would we. But the real problem is that we eat animals. Do you know how many animals we kill just in this country alone for food?"

"No. I am sure it's in the millions."

"It's in the billions. We kill about 14 billion in the U.S. alone and about 60 billion worldwide. That doesn't count fish. They're in the trillions."

"You don't eat fish either?"

"No. Our thinking is pretty simple. We can live a healthy life—I would say healthier life—without intentionally killing any animals. Why would we not do that?"

"Well, what do you eat?"

"Things that you eat, only more of some of those things and none of other things. You eat vegetables and fruits, right?"

"Sure. I love them."

"Good. Do you eat grains and beans?"

"I love those, too!"

"How about nuts and seeds? Do you like walnuts and cashews and sesame seeds and things like that?"

"Sure."

"Bingo, you can have a vegan diet with no problem. Just cut out everything else."

"And that's medically safe?"

"I am not a medical doctor but everything I've read says that a vegan diet is not only perfectly fine, but it may be even better than a diet that includes animal fats, which are linked to heart disease and cancer. And I can tell you that I feel great! Here, let me direct you to this website. It's something that we developed with a group of friends and it's all about going vegan. It's got recipes and everything."

Anna handed her a card that had www.howdoigovegan.com on it and she added:

"And by the way, our dogs are all vegans as well. This is Katie. She's 19 now—she may be older, actually, but she's at least 19. She's been a vegan since we got her 13 years ago."

"What do you feed them?"

"We use a commercial product called Evolution that is a very high-quality kibble product. We mix in vegetables, lentils, things like that. We have rescued a number of sick dogs over the years and they have all really flourished with a vegan diet."

"That's amazing. I never heard of that before. How about cats? Can they be vegans?"

"We've never lived with cats but we have many vegan friends who don't feed their cats meat. But I can tell you we have never had a dog who did not really thrive on a diet that had no animal products. The really important thing right now is that you see how easy it is for *you* to go vegan."

"You know, heart disease runs in my family."

"Well, all the more reason to get animal fats out of your diet. But the most important reason is what you said before—you said that you love animals and have loved them your whole life. Well, if you really love animals, killing and eating them when there's no need to do that isn't a good idea."

"Yes, I understand that."

"And there really isn't any difference between your dog and the cow or pig or chicken you eat."

"I don't each much beef or pork but I do eat a lot of chicken."

"People don't think of chickens as individuals. That's just because they're birds and we human mammals identify more with other mammals and less with birds, but chickens are wonderful little individuals as well. The point is that if you really do love animals, you shouldn't be eating any of them at all."

"And you don't drink milk or eat eggs either? They don't kill the animals for those things, right?"

"No, all animal products involve killing animals and all involve terrible suffering. Cows used for dairy are kept constantly pregnant and have their babies taken away from them, which causes great suffering for mother and baby. The calves are sold for veal and the moms end up in a slaughterhouse after about five years. Male chicks—that's 50% of them—are killed at birth and the hens are imprisoned in horrible circumstances irrespective of how supposedly "humane" it all is, and the hens are killed after one or two laying cycles anyway. Eggs are terrible. Milk is terrible. It's all really terrible. You love animals, right?"

"Very much."

"Well, harming them is not consistent with loving them."

Anna got called in to see the vet at that point. That entire exchange took approximately 7 minutes.

The key in situations like this is to be gentle and respectful and take your cues from the level of engagement of the other person. That person in this instance might feel "cornered" as they have to wait in the same area with you for their appointment, and they may be stressed as well because of the health condition of their animal companion. If you engage on matters they are willing to volunteer, or if you answer their questions, it softens the exchange because it does not make them defensive. It is just a conversation between two people who care about animals. The woman in this case got in touch with Anna for more information and several weeks after asking for that information, told Anna that she had gone vegan and needed information on where to get non-leather shoes.

## Sample Discussion: Harambe and Vegan Advocacy

In May 2016, after a small child entered an enclosure at the Cincinnati zoo that housed a silverback gorilla named Harambe, zoo officials shot and killed Harambe (https://goo.gl/FqkUvg). The outcry against the zoo officials and the mother of the child for allegedly failing to supervise him was deafening. But cases like this, along with situations in which lions or elephants are shot, or dolphins or whales killed, present a marvelous opportunity to engage in Abolitionist vegan education.

Here's a conversation that Gary had with a student:

Student: "Wasn't that business with Harambe terrible? I thought of you because it seems to be such a powerful animal rights case."

Gary: "Yes, it was awful. But he should not have been in the zoo in the first place."

"I suppose you're right. But I am just so upset about what happened. It's not fair that they shot him. It wasn't his fault. The poor thing did not deserve to die."

"I'm glad that you feel that way. You obviously are a caring person. But isn't what you think about Harambe true of all animals?"

"What do you mean?"

"Well, what did you have for dinner last night?"

"I had chicken. Why?"

"What is the difference between Harambe and that chicken you ate last night?"

"There's a difference."

"What is that difference apart from the fact that one animal is a chicken and one is a gorilla?"

"The gorilla is endangered, I think, or at least he was a more rare animal."

"But what difference does that make? Wouldn't you be as upset if Harambe were not endangered?"

"Yes, I suppose so."

"Obviously, you think that Harambe mattered. And you think that his life mattered—that he should not have died. The issue is why you think the chicken is any different."

"It feels like there was a difference. Harambe had a name."

"But that was just something that the humans who kept him imprisoned in the zoo called him. That was not his name. But your comment says something very important about how you are thinking about these issues."

"What's that, professor?"

"The fact that Harambe had a name made you see him as an individual. You saw him as some*one*, not some*thing*. But the chicken was someone, too. She just did not have a name."

"I never thought of it that way."

"Can you see that there is no difference between Harambe and the chicken in that the chicken valued her life as much as Harambe valued his? They both wanted to live. They were both killed by humans."

"Yes, I can see it. But isn't eating an animal different because you're doing that for nutrition?"

"Well, I'm not a physician or nutritionist but I can tell you that I've been vegan since 1982 and it's absolutely unnecessary to eat any animal products. Take a look at our website, www.howdoigo-vegan.com, and see what you think. Stop by if you want and we can talk more."

This was the beginning of a discussion that led a month later to the student becoming a vegan.

In such exchanges, try to slow the conversation down a little so that your listener can examine their own thoughts as the conversation progresses. If you keep the conversation going for a little while, you can push the person to go beyond their initial visceral reaction. As they begin to examine their reaction a little more closely, you give them some additional information that may guide them to a new perspective. Leave them with a friendly offer to answer any questions they may have in the future.

## Sample Discussion: "But I Love Animals"

A typical exchange:

"Oh, you're into animal rights. I love animals."

"I am glad that you love animals. But let me ask you: do you eat them?"

"Well, yes."

"How can you love animals if you actively participate in harming them?"

"Well, I have to eat."

"You certainly do, but you don't have to eat animals. There is absolutely no need to consume any animal products. Take a look at our website, www.howdoigovegan.com, and see what you think. Feel free to email us with any questions."

Even brief exchanges can be the start of a meaningful engagement concerning animal rights. A card with a website address is so helpful when time is short!

\*\*\*\*\*\*\*\*\*\*

In Chapter 6, we will discuss what to advocate from a different angle involving the rejection of "unnecessary" suffering.

# Chapter 6

## Veganism and Unnecessary Suffering and Death

### What Everyone Believes

As a general matter, people think that it is morally wrong to inflict unnecessary suffering on animals.

We've been doing animal work for 35 years now and we've met very few people who disagree with this. It is certainly accurate to say that this moral principle is very widely held. We can assure you that you can use it in your advocacy and get great results.

What does it mean to say that we should not impose unnecessary suffering on animals?

Well, if the principle has *any* meaning whatsoever, it must mean that we should not impose suffering on animals for reasons of pleasure, amusement, or convenience. If we are going to make animals suffer at all, we need a good reason. Pleasure, amusement, and convenience do not—*cannot*—constitute good reasons.

And that is exactly how people interpret it. People tend to react very strongly to situations in which people impose suffering on animals for the purpose of pleasure or amusement. For example, cruelty cases always evoke a strong public reaction. Stories about people torturing dogs, cats, or other companion animals always result in a great deal of publicity and calls for punishment. Most people—including those in Spain—oppose bullfighting. Most people—including conservatives in England—oppose fox hunting. And think about how strong the reaction was all over the world to Michael Vick, the American football player, who was involved in dog fighting.

If you don't believe us, ask the next five people you encounter: "Do you think it's okay for people to make animals suffer because they get some sort of pleasure or amusement out of it?" If all five don't respond that it is not okay and, indeed, ask you why you are asking such a bizarre question, please write to us immediately and let us know because we have *never* encountered such people.

Moreover, when people perceive the infliction of suffering to be unnecessary in that the suffering is justified only by pleasure, amusement, or convenience, such as in the case of dog fighting, they don't demand that the unnecessary suffering be made to be more humane; they demand that it should *stop*. The only time people talk about making animal treatment more "humane" is when they think that the use is necessary, and then, they want the treatment to involve as little suffering as possible.

Given that people agree that it's wrong to inflict unnecessary suffering on animals *and* they eat meat, dairy, eggs, etc., we can come to one clear conclusion: *people think it is necessary to consume animal products.*

If you are going to be an effective Abolitionist vegan advocate, you need to understand why people think that exploiting animals is necessary and how to educate them about why it is not necessary to do so. You need to convince them that their not being vegan means that they are doing exactly what they are accusing others of being cruel for doing: participating directly in the suffering and death of animals with no good reason. They are acting against what they claim to believe.

So let's start with the idea that people believe that it is unnecessary to impose unnecessary suffering and death on animals and ask: why do people believe that it is necessary to eat animals?

There are three primary reasons. You need to be able to address them all.

And you can.

## "Necessary" for Health

Many people still think that if they do not eat animal products, they will suffer ill health. This belief is probably *the* most significant barrier that we must address.

Many animal advocates do not understand that, despite there being an enormous amount of information indicating that consuming animal foods is not necessary for optimal human health, most people still believe that they will be unhealthy if they do not eat animal foods. Vegan advocates need to be ready to reply to this. After all, if people think that you are telling them that they have a moral obligation to do something that will harm them, they're not going to be interested.

*Your response:* You need to be clear: *no science-based organization* maintains that it's medically necessary to eat animal foods. All of the information you need is available at www.howdoigovegan.com.

As we make clear on that website, mainstream professional organizations across the world, including the Academy of Nutrition and Dietetics (U.S.), the American Diabetes Association, the American Heart Association, the British Dietetic Association, the British Nutritional Foundation, Dietician's Association of Australia, Dieticians of Canada, and the Heart and Stroke Foundation (U.S.); research and teaching institutions, including the Mayo Clinic, UCLA Health Center, University of Pennsylvania School of Medicine, and the University of Pittsburgh School of Medicine; governmental agencies, such as the British National Health Service, the U.S. National Institutes of Health, U.S. Department of Agriculture, and U.S. Department of Health and Human Services; and even large managed health care organizations, such as Kaiser Permanente, *all* acknowledge that a sound vegan diet is perfectly adequate for human health.

Some of these groups claim that vegan diets may have significant health benefits over diets containing animal products. But you don't have to convince anyone of that in order to make your primary point: that it is not necessary to consume animal foods. Those who stop eating animals and who adopt a sensible vegan diet won't be any less healthy. They may be *more* healthy but they certainly won't be any *less* healthy.

In any event, you need to assure them that vegans can get *everything* they need from plants: protein, calcium, iron, zinc, etc. Vegans have to make sure they get vitamin B-12, which humans do not manufacture, or at least not in reliable quantities. But all humans have to get B-12 from somewhere. Nonvegans get it from meat; vegans get it from nutritional yeast, other fortified food, or supplements. But *all* B-12 comes from microorganisms. Vegans just get theirs more directly from plant sources—just as do the animals.

Humans also need fatty acids that they don't manufacture. Most people get their essential fatty acids from eating fish. The fish get it from consuming algae. Vegans get these fatty acids directly from an algae supplement. As in the case of B-12, vegans get their fatty acids from the same place that the animals that others eat get theirs. They're just more efficient! Vegans can also eat flaxseeds and walnuts, which provide these nutrients.

So while there is considerable evidence that animal foods are detrimental to human health, it isn't necessary to get into a battle of medical studies here to convince people that it's healthier not to eat animal products. All you need to do is to convince people that it's as healthy to be a vegan as it is to be a nonvegan.

You need to educate yourself *not* so that you can give dietary or medical advice, which, if you are not qualified to do so, you should never do in any case. Rather, you need to be conversant with the basics and able to point people to sources where they can get information to disabuse themselves of the very incorrect notion that animal products are required for optimal human health.

As mentioned earlier, our website, www.howdoigovegan.com, has information about health and nutrition, including links to professional and governmental bodies that make clear that animal products are not required for optimal health, and some Abolitionist vegan advocates carry cards (the size of a business card) that have the URL of the site. We know some advocates who have had the website URL printed on inexpensive pens that they hand out to people and some who give people the website of vegan body builders so that people can see that vegans can build muscles as well as anyone!

Note: You should not give anyone particular medical or nutritional advice unless you are qualified to do so. You should limit your discussion to providing publicly available materials for them to review.

## "Necessary" Because "Natural"

Related to the concern about health is the idea that consuming animals is necessary because it is "natural." Many people think that if we don't eat animals, we are acting against nature because we are physically adapted to eat meat and other animal products.

*Your response:* The fact that we are omnivores and we can eat animal foods as well as plant foods does not answer the moral question of whether it is moral to do so.

It is important to emphasize that, in addition to many people being lactose intolerant and the undisputable fact that many physicians are pointing out that animal products are detrimental to human health, the *most* we can say is that we *can* eat animal products; there is nothing about our bodies that suggests that our bodies are designed to require them.

Humans compare physically much more to herbivores than to carnivores. Carnivores have well-developed claws. We don't have claws. We also lack the sharp front teeth carnivorous animals need. Although we still have canine teeth, they are not sharp and cannot be used in the way carnivorous animals use their sharp canine teeth. We have flat molar teeth, which are similar to those of many herbivores, and that we, like those herbivores, use for grinding.

Carnivores have a short intestinal tract so that they can quickly expel decaying meat. Herbivores have a much longer intestinal tract as do humans. Herbivores and humans have weak stomach acid relative to carnivores who have strong hydrochloric acid in their stomachs to digest meat.

Herbivorous animals have well-developed salivary glands for pre-digesting fruits and grains and have alkaline saliva that is needed to pre-digest grains, as do humans. Carnivorous animals tend to have acidic saliva.

So if we look at the physiology, it would appear that we are better adapted to eat plants than animal products.

## "Necessary" Because We've Been Doing it Forever

Many people are just overwhelmed when they think about not eating what they've been eating all their lives. They think of what they have been doing all their lives as *necessary.* They often become anxious when they contemplate what they see as a significant change. It overwhelms them. This is not an unusual phenomenon. For example, moving house—even when people are excited to move—is stressful. So it's not unexpected that people will experience stress if they contemplate a radical change in their diet.

*Your response:* You need to assure them that going vegan is easy. And, for the vast majority of people, it is. Unfortunately, as we saw earlier, many of the large animal welfare corporations make a habit of promoting veganism as difficult. Show them it's not difficult at all.

Emphasize to people that eating vegan means nothing more than eating vegetables, fruits, grains, beans, seeds, and nuts. Everyone has eaten these foods before. Everyone eats some of them now, even if they also eat animal foods. They are just going to eat more of what they are already eating. There's nothing scary. There's nothing weird.

And it's not expensive. We frequently hear people expressing anxiety that it is expensive to go vegan.

It is crucial to emphasize that people don't have to purchase expensive, prepared vegan products. That is, they don't have to substitute, for example, vegan "hamburgers" for hamburgers. Many vegans eat very few prepared foods. We have found that, in addition to being very expensive, they're full of salt and have little nutritive value.

The mantra: vegetables, fruits, grains, beans, seeds, and nuts. These foods are familiar to everyone and everyone has already consumed them. Always emphasize: *easy, easy, easy.* That's because it *is* easy.

You should always be able to point people to sites where they can get recipes—going from very simple to formal dinner party grade. Again, www.howdoigovegan.com seeks to provide that information but there are many other sources of vegan recipes.

We will revisit dealing with the extremely anxious person in greater detail in Chapter 10.

## Sample Discussion: A General Consideration of "Necessity"

In 2014, a young man in New York, Andre Robinson, kicked a cat as one would kick a football. A video that was made of the incident by someone who was there was posted on YouTube and went viral. Robinson did not kill the cat, who was adopted into a good home. Robinson was charged with animal cruelty and the case generated a frenzied campaign by "animal lovers" who wanted Robinson to be imprisoned for what he did.

Gary was interviewed on CNN, a cable-news network in the United States. He was asked, as a professor who teaches criminal law, whether Robinson should be imprisoned. He expressed the view that he thought the campaign against Robinson, a man of color, had disturbingly racist overtones. But his main point was that Robinson had engaged in harming an animal because he got pleasure from it; he thought it was "fun." Gary said that the people calling for Robinson's punishment were discussing what a bad person Robinson was as they sat eating their hamburgers and other animal foods. That is, they were participating directly in imposing harm on nonhuman animals and the best justification that they had was that animals tasted good. He argued that those people were really no different from Robinson.

Needless to say, this interview, although brief, generated a fair amount of controversy. Here is a transcript of a text discussion that Gary had with another person, an academic at another university. She agreed to let her texts be used as we are not disclosing any names in sharing these discussions.

Colleague: "I saw your interview on CNN. Do you mind answering some questions?"

Gary: "No, of course not."

"So you think the reaction was racist?"

"Sure it was. There was a great deal of overtly racist commentary online on the pages of people who were leading the charge against Robinson. But I certainly don't think that racism accounted entirely for the reaction."

"Good, because I think what he did was wrong and I don't consider myself racist."

"Why do you object to what he did?"

"Because it was wrong to kick the cat."

"But why was it wrong?"

"That's obvious."

"Okay, tell me why then."

"Because it was gratuitous. It was cruel. It served no purpose."

"That's not true. Robinson got enjoyment out of it."

"Sure, but that can't be sufficient."

"Why not?"

"Because you need a good reason to harm an animal."

"He had a reason—he got pleasure from it."

"But that's not a good reason."

"Why not?"

"For real?"

"Yes, for real. Why is his pleasure or amusement not sufficient?"

"Because we require that there be a need beyond that to justify killing an animal/making the animal suffer."

"Let me ask you a question: are you a vegan?"

"No."

"Well, how are you any different from Andre Robinson?"

"???"

"I misspoke. Why are you not worse than Robinson?"

"??????"

"Robinson didn't kill the cat—you're participating directly in the killing of animals by not being a vegan."

"Totally different."

"How?"

"I don't actually kill any animal."

"That may be but you are still paying someone else to do it."

"True."

"There's no difference just as there would be no difference morally or legally if you kill someone or pay someone else to do it for you."

"Agreed. But there's a difference. I support animal use for nutrition. That's different from Robinson."

"But you don't have to eat animal products to be optimally healthy."

"That's controversial."

"No, it's not. No one maintains that you need to eat animal products; if anything, there's mounting evidence that eating animal products is not good for you."

"Can you send me some references?"

"Sure. And here's a website that I designed with a group of creative vegans: www.howdoigovegan.com."

"Thanks. I'll take a look."

"Good. Come back to me with any questions."

"I worry about osteoporosis. It runs in my family."

"As the website will explain to you, you're far more likely to get that sort of problem if you eat animal products, including milk."

"I will have to look."

"But do you see the point that if animal products are not necessary for human health, you are no different morally from Robinson—

except you're worse!"

"Yes, I see it. I really need to see that evidence on nutrition. I thought you needed animal protein."

"I haven't had any in going on 35 years. I feel great."

"I'll be interested to see what you send. You've raised an interesting position I've not heard before. I better understand what you said on CNN."

Gary had several further exchanges with this person. She is now a vegan.

## Sample Discussion: Vegan—It's Natural

Anna had the following discussion with a man who attended a lecture we both gave at a conference. The discussion occurred after the lecture when the person came up to ask a question. What follows is based on notes that were jotted down after the event.

Person: "I understand what you're saying about veganism but I think that there's a dimension that you're leaving out."

Anna: "What's that?"

"Being a vegan is not natural."

"What do you mean by that, 'not natural'?"

"We were meant to eat animals."

"Meant by whom?"

"Nature."

"What does that mean?"

"We're designed to eat meat."

"What part of our bodies makes you think that?"

"Our teeth."

"But our teeth are more like those of herbivores. Our teeth cannot rip raw flesh from a bone. Our intestines are much longer than those of a carnivore and our stomach acids are more amenable to digesting vegetables and fruits than meat."

"But we've been eating animals since prehistoric times."

"There's actually controversy about ancient diets but it doesn't matter. We've been doing many things for a long time, like waging war and oppressing women. What matters is whether we can morally justify imposing suffering and death on animals and I hope we convinced you that there is no good justification."

"It was an interesting lecture for sure but our use of animals seems to be really part of who we are."

"But the same thing could be said about sexism, for instance. It's a part of what men have been for thousands of years! And some men have actually tried to justify patriarchy that way."

"I understand. Thanks a lot. It was very interesting."

Three months later, Anna heard from the person that he had gone vegan.

## A Note on Vivisection

The *only* time that we can *arguably* say that it is "necessary" to use animals is in the context of using animals to solve serious human health problems. We reject animal use there as well, but our rejection involves a discussion of rights concepts, which we will review in the next chapter.

# Chapter 7

## Veganism and Animal Rights

Many animal advocates get very anxious when they think about advocating for animal rights and, in particular, the right not to be property, which is a central Abolitionist concept.

Don't get anxious! You don't need a law degree or training in philosophy to talk about rights.

For the purpose of doing Abolitionist vegan advocacy, you need to understand two simple concepts:

- The concept of a right

- Why the Abolitionist Approach is built on the idea of a right not to be property

Let's look at each of these and we'll see how simple these ideas are.

# Rights

There has been a great deal written about the concept of rights. Thankfully, we don't have to worry about 99.9999% of it in order to talk with others about animal rights.

- A right is a way of protecting an interest.

- An interest is something we prefer, desire, or want.

- To have that interest protected by a right is simply to say that the interest must be respected even if others would benefit by not respecting it.

That's it. That's all you need. Let's explore in a simple way what this means.

There are two ways to protect an interest. The first way is to protect it only to the extent that protecting it produces desirable consequences. The second way is to protect it despite considerations of consequences. If we protect an interest in this second way—that is, we protect it even if it would generate good consequences if we did not protect it—we can be said to protect the interest with a *right*.

Here's an example: You have an interest in your life. You prefer, desire, or want to stay alive. Your interest is protected by a right. That means simply that others must respect your interest in continuing to live and not kill you even if killing you would benefit other people. So, even if your organs could be used to save the lives of five people, all of whom are important scientists who will die without organ transplants, we still protect your interest in not being used as a forced organ donor. We protect your interest with a right—*a right to life*.

Here's another example. You have an interest in your freedom—in doing what you want as long as you don't harm others. We protect your interest in your liberty (although we often interpret what will harm others in a very broad way) unless you do something (e.g., commit a crime) even if others would benefit from our restricting your liberty. For example, a brutal murder is committed. People are very upset and frightened. No one will leave their homes to go to work. The economy grinds to a halt. The police know for a fact that the murderer was killed in an automobile accident but they know that no one will believe them, and that the public will continue to fear. So the police falsely announce that an innocent person is the murderer, and that person is imprisoned.

The public is reassured and life goes back to normal. None of us would think that is morally acceptable to treat an innocent person in this way. That person has a *right to liberty* and this means that their interest in their liberty will be protected even if abrogating their liberty will have many benefits.

See? It's very simple.

The application of this simple concept to the context of animal ethics is also simple. Let's move on to the second idea: the concept of property and the right to not be used as property.

## Humans and Animals as Property

We all agree—however much we may disagree about what moral rights humans have—that all humans must have a moral right not to be chattel slaves. Why is that? Because if a human is a chattel slave, then that human is not considered to be a being who matters morally—a *person*— but is only a *thing* that has economic value that is determined by the owner of the slave.

We all recognize that if a human is going to count morally at all, they must have the right not to be property; their interest in not being a thing must be protected by a right so that their interest in not being a mere thing is respected even if others would benefit from not respecting it. In other words, even if you would benefit greatly from treating John as a thing and enslaving John, you can't do so.

A right to not be used as property is the very minimum level of protection you need to matter morally. If you don't have this right— if your interest in not being used as a resource that has no value is not recognized—then you *will* be used as a resource whenever people believe that they will benefit from doing so.

The same reasoning holds for nonhuman animals. If they are going to matter morally, and not be just things, they cannot, by the simple application of logic, be property. If they are property, then they have no moral value. Their value is that which is accorded to them by their owners.

We extend the right not to be property to *all* humans, irrespective of particular characteristics, such as level of intelligence or any mental attribute, beauty, strength, etc. It does not matter whether a human is a genius or is mentally disabled. We don't think anyone should be the property of another.

The only reason we deny this same right to all nonhumans is that they are not members of the human species. But that is no different from denying this right to others based on race, sex, sexual orientation/ preference/identification, etc.

Therefore, we are morally committed to recognizing that all sentient nonhumans (non-sentient beings cannot have interests in the first place) have a moral right not to be used as property and this requires that we stop using animals as resources. In other words, we are morally committed to stop eating, wearing, or otherwise using animals as human resources.

There's a great deal more that we could say about rights. Indeed, in other places, such as our book, *Animal Rights: The Abolitionist Approach*, we've done just that. But for our purposes here, we've laid out everything you need to know to engage people about how animal rights *means* veganism.

## Issues That Come Up

There are three issues that almost always come up in discussions of rights within an Abolitionist perspective.

*First,* people often think that "animal rights" means that we ought to accord to animals the legal rights held by humans.

No one is saying that animals should have a right to drive or a right to vote or a right to own a house. The *only* right that is at issue is the right not to be used as property and thereby under the absolute control of the property owner. If this one right were recognized and respected, it would require the abolition of *all* institutionalized animal use and this would necessitate the end of *all* domestication.

Recognition of this one right would not mean that there would be no more conflicts between humans and nonhumans. There would still be non-domesticated animals living remotely from humans in woods and jungles, as well as those who live amongst us, such as squirrels, rabbits, rats, mice, birds, and many other creatures. We would still need a framework to deal with those nonhumans but, if we recognized that we could no longer engage in the exploitation of any nonhuman domesticates, the chances that we would be able to develop a solid framework would be maximized.

Do Abolitionists regard the right not to be used as a legal right? Yes and no.

No, in that the law will never prohibit the institutionalized exploitation of nonhuman animals until there are a sizeable number of people who have embraced the rejection of the property status of animals as a moral principle. The law rarely, if ever, initiates a paradigm shift. As a general matter, the law follows moral change. So it is simply not realistic to believe that the Supreme Court is going to declare animals "persons" under the law, or that Congress is going to legislate the end of institutionalized animal use, until there are lots and lots of people who believe that animal use—however supposedly "humane"—is morally wrong.

But yes, in that Abolitionists look forward to the day when the moral paradigm has shifted and animals will get their personhood recognized by law.

*Second,* many people think that because animals do not recognize and respect human rights, humans are under no obligation to recognize that animals have rights.

This is a most peculiar argument but it is easy to rebut.

There are many humans who do not or cannot recognize or respect the rights of other humans: infants, young children, those with some mental disabilities, etc. Even if we think it is appropriate to deny these humans some rights, such as the right to drive, or make contracts, or vote, do we think it is acceptable to deny them the right not to be used as things? Of course not. Why? Because the right not to be used as things does not depend on anything they do or don't do. It is based on their *status* as *persons*—as beings who matter morally, as beings who are not just things. In other words, if they matter morally, we cannot use them as things whether or not they recognize or respect human rights.

*Third,* people often ask whether rights are necessary and whether we could better protect animals even if they remain property. The answer is that we could do so but there are powerful economic incentives against doing so. It costs money to protect animal interests and the more we protect those interests, the more expensive it becomes and someone— usually the consumer—has to pay that expense. And however supposedly "humanely" the animal is treated, the animal will still be killed and, as Abolitionists, we reject that. The *only* way to recognize the moral personhood of animals is to accord them a right not to be property—and that means the *end* of domestication.

## Discussion Example

Here is a discussion that we recently had with someone at a talk we were giving:

> Person at talk: "I am confused about what it means to say that animals have rights. How can animals have rights?"
>
> Us: "We're talking about one right—a right not to be used as property."
>
> "So you're not saying that they have the same rights humans do?"
>
> "No, of course not."
>
> "But what does it mean to say that they have even that one right?"
>
> "Think about it this way. We think that every human has the right not to be property."
>
> "Yes, we reject slavery."
>
> "And why is that?"
>
> "Because slavery is wrong."
>
> "But why is it wrong?"
>
> "I've never really thought about how to put that into words before. I guess it is because if someone is a slave, someone else gets to control and use them. It's the ultimate denial of moral value."
>
> "Yes, that's right. Their owner gets to decide their value. A human can't be a slave and have any moral value; a human who is enslaved is just a thing."
>
> "Yes. I agree with that."

"Now, if it would benefit me very much for you to be my slave, would it be okay to enslave you?"

"No, of course not."

"What if it would benefit thousands of people if you were made to be a slave. Would it be okay then?"

"No. It wouldn't matter how many people benefited."

"Why wouldn't it matter?"

"Because I have a right not to be a slave."

"Exactly. See, you understand this very clearly. If you are going to matter morally at all, you can't be a slave. And the consequences of enslaving you don't matter. You have an interest in not being slaved that should be protected irrespective of consequences."

"Yes, that's correct."

"And that is another way of saying that you have a right not to be property."

"Okay, yes, I am with you so far."

"The same thinking applies to animals. Animals are property. They are just things. They don't matter morally. If they are going to matter morally, they can't be property. If they are property, they just have an economic value—they have no other value."

"Yes, but animals are different from humans."

"Different how?"

"Well, to begin with, they don't recognize our rights."

"But little children, some people who are mentally disabled, and elderly people with dementia may not recognize our rights either. So what? Does that mean it is okay to treat them like slaves and use them as forced organ donors or as unwilling subjects in biomedical experiments?"

"No, it doesn't."

"There is not one single 'defect' that animals supposedly have where that 'defect' is not also possessed by some group of humans. But we would never treat such humans as things. The only difference between humans and nonhumans is species, and species alone is morally irrelevant in the same way that race, sex, sexual orientation/preference, etc alone are morally irrelevant for determining who has moral value and who is used exclusively as a resource, as a thing."

"You use the expression, 'nonhuman person' a lot. What does that mean?"

"By 'person,' we mean someone who has moral value, as opposed to a thing, which has no moral value and only has the external or extrinsic value that we accord it. It's a binary world. There are things, which have only the value we accord them, and persons, who have inherent value. Up to this point, we have thought that only humans are persons. The Abolitionist Approach maintains that nonhumans are persons as well; they aren't just things. They have moral value, but in order to have moral value, we must protect their interest in not being a thing even if the consequences would be beneficial to us. That's simply another way of saying that we should recognize the right of nonhumans to not be things; to not be property; to be persons."

"Okay, but if I recognize that animals have rights, what does that mean in terms of my conduct?"

"Given that our exploitation of animals—our use of them as food, clothing, etc.—rests on their being our property, if we recognize that animals have a moral right not to be treated as property, we can no longer exploit them. If nonhuman animals are persons, then we are committed to veganism."

"Do we have to wait until this right is a legal right?"

"No. It will become recognized by law only if it is widely accepted as a moral principle. That is, unless and until many people embrace ethical veganism as their recognition of the right of animals not to be property, there will be no recognition of the right under the law."

We have included this conversation script to show you that you can explain these important concepts that underpin the Abolitionist

Approach. This framework is powerful because it rests on concepts and understanding that we already have—they are concepts that already function in our everyday lives and thinking.

If you familiarize yourself with this simple way of discussing such important concepts, you will gain the confidence to introduce the concepts into your advocacy discussions. Do it again and again until you can effectively work through these ideas with others.

\*\*\*\*\*\*\*\*\*\*

In the next chapter, we will consider how to discuss veganism with other "animal advocates" who are not Abolitionist and who reject veganism as a moral baseline.

# Chapter 8

## Talking with Other "Animal Advocates" Who Reject Veganism as a Moral Baseline

Most animal advocates reject the Abolitionist position promoted in this book. Indeed, the Abolitionist position is rejected by every large corporate animal charity and by many of the people who support those charities. Many of these "animal advocates" are actually hostile to the Abolitionist position.

In fact, it's much easier to talk about veganism as a moral obligation with people who care about animals but who have nothing to do with these large animal charities than it is to talk with the leaders, employees, or supporters of these charities.

The bottom line is that all "animal advocates" who are not Abolitionists reject the idea that veganism is a moral obligation—that is, they reject the idea that we have a moral obligation to go vegan and they reject the idea that, if a person is not a vegan, that person is participating directly in animal exploitation. Most of them claim that it's great if someone does go vegan, but they are very clear that no one is under a moral obligation to go vegan. People can be "compassionate" and "help the animals" even if they are not vegan.

These "animal advocates" promote animal welfare reform that will result in supposedly more "humane" exploitation. For example, they promote enriched-cage or cage-free eggs rather than eggs from conventional battery cages. They encourage consumers to buy crate-free pork rather than pork from animals who have been confined in gestation crates.

They promote "reducetarian" campaigns that encourage people to reduce their consumption of animal products. For example, they promote things like "Meatless Monday," "Vegan Before 6 p.m.," and campaigns to encourage people to eat cows, pigs, and other larger animals, rather than chickens, more of whom have to be raised and killed to feed the same number of humans. They promote "flexible" veganism. Indeed, Peter Singer, author of Animal Liberation, calls himself a "flexible" vegan because he will eat animal products when traveling or in the homes of others.

They promote single-issue campaigns that target particular sorts of animal exploitation, such as fur or foie gras production, or the consumption of dog meat in some Asian countries.

## Three Reasons That Don't Work

Why do these "animal advocates" promote these sorts of efforts rather than promoting the idea that veganism is the only rational response to the recognition that animals matter morally?

They usually give three reasons. *None* of them works. *All* of them are speciesist.

### *"But we won't get everyone to go vegan overnight!"*

Non-Abolitionist "animal advocates" claim that Abolitionists are not realistic and that we cannot end animal exploitation "overnight" (a position that no Abolitionist maintains) so we should focus instead on reducing animal suffering "now." They claim that their welfare campaigns, reducetarian campaigns, and single-issue campaigns reduce suffering and do so immediately.

Abolitionists reject such campaigns because they are transparently speciesist in that they encourage people to continue to participate in animal exploitation. If it is wrong to exploit animals, then it is wrong to promote supposedly "humane" exploitation, reduced exploitation, or to arbitrarily target particular sorts of exploitation. Less suffering is certainly better than more suffering, but where fundamental human rights violations are involved, we recognize that it is wrong to promote any occurrences of those violations. That is, we all agree that a rape that also involves physical torture is worse than a rape that does not involve it, but we would never support a campaign for less violent rape because we think that it is morally odious to promote *any* occurrences of rape as morally good.

But that is *exactly* what happens when "animal advocates" promote "happy" exploitation. When, for example, these large animal groups campaign for cage-free eggs or crate-free pork, they are *necessarily* saying to the public that consuming those products is a morally good thing. They are *encouraging* animal exploitation. When companies agree to switch from a conventional battery cage to an enriched cage or to cage-free production, or to make chicken production more "humane," and the animal charities praise these actions publicly, they are putting a stamp of approval on continued animal exploitation irrespective of whatever else the animal charities say. These "animal advocates" are, in essence, *promoting* animal exploitation. We would never think that to be appropriate in the human context but it is done constantly by "animal advocates" in the nonhuman context.

Let us look at an example. On the website of Bells and Evans, an industrial-scale poultry supplier, the following statement from Ingrid Newkirk of People for the Ethical Treatment of Animals appears: "Bell & Evans shows that animal welfare and good business can go hand in hand. ...and by listening to consumers' wishes, Bell & Evans has set a new standard for the chicken-supply industry." (https://goo.gl/fktZoR)

How is this not PETA putting a stamp of approval on animal exploitation? It clearly and indisputably is. How is this any different from promoting "higher welfare" violations of fundamental human rights? It clearly and indisputably isn't.

The same analysis applies to the various reducetarian strategies promoted by "animal people." That is, in the face of violence against women or children would anyone seriously promote reducing this violence as a morally good thing? Would anyone promote "Rape-free Monday" or reducing one's racist epithets as a good thing? Again, if

John is a racist and makes twenty racists statements per week, it is a better thing if John drops to ten a week but it is not a good thing that he is making *any* racist statements. No one would promote reduced instances of racist behavior as a morally good thing in the way that "animal people" promote reducing consumption as something that is a morally acceptable alternative to veganism. "Less bad" is not acceptable when a simple "good" is easily achievable.

When "animal advocates" target fur, they necessarily imply (and sometimes state explicitly) that fur is morally distinguishable from wool or leather, which is not the case. When "animal advocates" target foie gras, they necessarily imply (and sometimes state explicitly) that there is a morally coherent distinction between foie gras and any other animal product. There isn't.

Abolitionists reject the idea that making animal exploitation supposedly more "humane" does anything to help animals "now." Animal welfare reforms, whether imposed by law or the result of voluntary industry agreement, are almost never immediate. They are usually phased in over a period of years and they are almost always subject to multiple exceptions. They do nothing to help animals *now.*

Moreover, because making animal exploitation supposedly more "humane" actually encourages people to continue to consume animals, welfare reform and single-issue campaigns may *increase* net suffering precisely because this approach says to people who care that, if they care, they don't have to stop exploiting animals; they can continue to exploit animals as long as they exploit more compassionately. If people stop buying fur, they will simply buy more wool and leather. People who stop eating foie gras don't eat tofu instead. They simply switch to another animal product that is morally indistinguishable— except they feel better about it morally. People who don't eat meat on Meatless Monday eat more eggs and dairy. There is no morally coherent distinction between meat and other animal products. That is why vegetarianism is an incoherent position to take. It is like saying that you don't eat the meat from brown cows but do eat the meat from spotted cows.

The creative, nonviolent vegan advocacy that is promoted by Abolitionists has the immediate effect of reducing demand. Although demand will not be affected by one person going vegan, a number of people going vegan over the time that it takes welfare reforms to be implemented can have an effect on demand. Moreover, those who stop eating, wearing, and using animals no longer go to circuses, rodeos, zoos, and aquaria, and do not patronize other forms of animal exploitation.

So the choice is not between helping animals now or not, but between perpetuating demand or decreasing demand over the longer term.

Abolitionists also point out that the level of "humane" treatment accorded to animals will always be low because animals are property and, as such, it costs money to protect animal interests. The most "humanely" produced animal products involve animals whose lives and deaths would be considered as involving torture were humans involved. The laying hen in a conventional barn, the one in a cage-free barn, and the one in a free-range situation are all subjected to a life that has pain and distress, and they all end up in the same slaughterhouse.

### *"But veganism is 'extreme.'"*

Non-Abolitionist "animal advocates" claim that we cannot educate people about veganism because that is too "radical" or "extreme." Rather, we have to get people to take "baby steps" and, therefore, we need to encourage them to eat cage-free eggs, or to reduce their consumption of animal products, or to go vegetarian, as steps toward veganism. They will often say that they did not go vegan immediately and went on a "journey" that lasted, in some cases, for many years, before they went vegan. Therefore, veganism cannot be a matter of a moral obligation. Rather, at most, we are just obligated to "try" to stop participating directly in the exploitation of animals, but continuing to participate in animal exploitation is morally acceptable.

Once again, this is speciesist—and silly.

If someone reported that they had been raised as a racist and that it took them years to stop being racist, would we say that it is acceptable to promote the idea that people don't have an obligation to reject racism and that it's fine for people to think about rejecting racism as a matter of their being on a "journey?" Of course not. The fact that it may take us time to recognize that we have been acting wrongly in violating the fundamental rights of others does not mean that it is morally acceptable to promote continuing to engage in those rights violations as a moral matter because we are on some sort of "journey." We would never do that where human rights are involved. We should not do that where nonhumans are involved.

It is no surprise that most people did not go vegan immediately. After all, most people came to the animal issue by getting involved with one of the large animal charities—none of which promotes veganism as a moral obligation and all of which tell people that they can satisfy their moral obligations to animals without going vegan. Those who go vegan immediately do so in the face of "experts" who tell them that there is no need for them to do so.

Related to the "baby steps" position is the position that we can't talk about veganism as a moral obligation because people are just not smart enough to understand that idea. Indeed, Gary had the experience of debating a founding member of one of the large British animal charities who declared—publicly—that "single mums" were not likely to appreciate the idea that veganism was a moral obligation. We disagree and find such positions to be offensive. Indeed, our experience has been that *everyone* can understand the message of Abolitionist veganism. Ironically, it's only some "animal advocates" who seem to have a problem.

### *"But no one can be a vegan!"*

Non-Abolitionist "animal advocates" claim that, because there are animal ingredients in plastics, road surfaces, etc., we cannot really be vegan and should not characterize veganism as a moral obligation because it is an obligation that no one can satisfy. This position indicates an ignorance of what veganism means as a moral position. As we saw in the Introduction, veganism means not participating in animal exploitation to the extent *practicable*. Where one cannot choose in a meaningful way, avoidance of animal products is not practicable. Because we kill so many animals and because animal by-products are so cheap, they are everywhere and in everything. As a practical matter, they cannot be avoided. The solution: veganism. If we all stopped exploiting animals, those by-products would no longer be available.

A related position is that animals are harmed in crop production so even if we are not eating, wearing, or using animals, we are still the cause of animals dying. But that is no different from saying, for example, that because humans are unintentionally or incidentally injured in the process of producing goods, there is no difference between buying goods and murdering people. There is a difference between deliberate harm—harm in which we participate directly and intentionally—and harm that is not deliberate or intended. When I take a gun and shoot a person, I have deliberately harmed that person. When I build a road and a person dies from driving on that road (and I know with certainty when I build the road that some number of people will die or be injured on the road), there is a difference between that death and the death I would cause if I shot that person. Humans are harmed all the time in the processes that result in making the products we consume, but there is a clear difference between shooting a person and buying a product that involved an industrial accident in which a person was harmed. To say that we can continue to participate directly in the exploitation of nonhuman animals because we cannot avoid harm to them when we would *never* say that in the human context is speciesist.

There is a difference between the unintended and incidental harm to animals harmed in growing plants, and deliberately exploiting animals, treating them as commodities, and killing them to use as resources. It should also be noted that raising animals for food involves not only killing those animals, but also killing all the animals that die as part of the crop production process, and it takes many more pounds of plant to produce animal products that it would if we consumed those plants directly. So if we are vegans, we are not only not participating in the deliberate harm of sentient beings, but we are also responsible for many fewer unintended and incidental deaths that occur as a result of the agricultural process.

## Non-Abolitionist "Animal Advocacy": The *Real* Reason

The real reason that accounts for why those involved in or with the corporate animal charities do not promote veganism as a moral baseline is not usually stated—at least publicly—but is probably the most important reason of all. Simply put: animal charities need donations and it's easier to get donations, and to get them from a larger group of people, if you don't challenge anyone and take the position that veganism is a moral baseline. It's easier to get people who eat animals to donate to a campaign that will supposedly make animal exploitation more "humane" and stop the "abuses." It's easier to get donations from people who eat meat, dairy, and eggs by getting them to hate the Chinese or Koreans who eat dogs or the Japanese who kill whales and dolphins. It's easier to get donations from people who wear wool by getting them to hate people who wear fur.

We discuss the problem with animal welfare charities at length in *Animal Rights: The Abolitionist Approach* and in essays on our website, www.abolitionistapproach.com. For purposes of our discussion here, when talking with animal advocates who promote campaigns for "humane" exploitation, reducetarianism, etc., we suggest you ask a simple question: *Would you promote such a campaign if there were a violation of the fundamental rights of humans involved?* Most animal advocates who oppose Abolition do not have a good answer for this question because there is no answer that does not expose the speciesism of their position.

## Sample Discussion: Meatless Monday

Here is an example of a discussion focusing on Meatless Monday. We frequently have these sorts of discussions with welfarist advocates.

Welfarist: "Why don't you support the Meatless Monday campaign?"

Abolitionist: "Because it is speciesist."

"How so?"

"First of all, you're perpetuating the idea that meat is morally distinguishable from milk and eggs."

"Yes, but it reduces suffering if people give up meat on Monday."

"Really? Most people who participate in this campaign will simply eat more dairy, or more eggs, to make up for not eating meat. I know people who eat fish on Meatless Monday."

"Yes, but it helps to get people thinking about the issue of not eating animal products."

"No, it's just getting them to focus on eating other animal products. But let me ask you a question: how is Meatless Monday not speciesist?"

"What do you mean?"

"Would you have a 'Racist-Joke-Free Day' to address racism?"

"No."

"Good. Would you have a 'Less-Brutal Rape Monday'?"

"No. But rape is already against the law."

"Right but it is still a serious problem in that it occurs very frequently despite it being illegal. Maybe we need to take a more incremental approach."

"No. That would not be right because it would suggest that brutal rapes are okay on Tuesday."

"Exactly. That is a precise analogy to the message you are promoting."

## Sample Discussion: Cage-Free Eggs

Many welfarists promote cage-free eggs as a "baby step" to help animals. Here is an example of a typical discussion involving this issue. This approach can be used with any welfarist "baby step."

Welfarist: "I am supporting the campaign to get [Company X] to buy all of their eggs from cage-free producers."

Abolitionist: "Why don't you just promote veganism?"

"Because we have to do something to help animals now."

"Well, *even if* you think that cage-free eggs are an improvement over conventional battery cages, have you looked to see what the time line will be?"

"No."

"These sorts of 'improvements' are always phased in over a period of many years and there are all sorts of exceptions. They do nothing to help animals *now*. But there's an additional problem."

"What's that?"

"The entire campaign is speciesist."

"How so?"

"You're promoting the idea that consuming these eggs is a morally good thing to do."

"But less suffering is better than more, isn't it?"

"Yes, but that does not mean that we should promote consuming the product of less suffering as a good thing."

"What do you mean?"

"Well, it's better if I am going to murder you that I do not torture

127

you first, right?"

"Yes."

"But would we promote murder without torture as a good thing?"

"No."

"Even if a cage-free barn is better than a conventional cage, the birds are still tortured, don't you agree?"

"Yes."

"And they still end up dead."

"Yes."

"Then, if we believe that animals matter morally, we ought not to promote eating any eggs, cage-free, free-range, conventional cage, 'enriched' cage, etc."

## Sample Discussion: "People Won't Go Vegan Overnight"

The most commonly used welfarist argument against the Abolitionist position is to claim that people won't go vegan immediately so we ought not to advocate veganism as a moral imperative. Here is a sample discussion in which that position is addressed.

Welfarist: "The problem with you Abolitionists is that you don't understand that people won't go vegan overnight."

Abolitionist: "Some people will go vegan as soon as someone explains the argument about why veganism is a moral imperative."

"But some won't."

"Yes, that's correct. Some won't."

"Well, those are the people who really need to be encouraged to take steps, such as reducing their consumption of animal products or eating cage-free eggs rather than conventional eggs."

"As an Abolitionist, I disagree with that approach."

"Why? If it's about animals and not about you, shouldn't you encourage them to take steps?"

"It's very much about the animals and nothing about me. But I would never tell people that their eating any quantity of any animal products is a morally good thing."

"But isn't less harm better than more?"

"Sure it is, but we should never encourage people to engage in harming others. Think about it in the human context. It's better if a person rapes a victim less violently than more violently, but we would never promote the less violent rape as a good thing—as something that people ought to do."

"Of course not."

"Well, then, why would we do that in the animal context? Indeed, to do so would be speciesist. Telling people that they ought to eat 'happy' eggs or consume fewer animal products is tantamount to encouraging them to continue to exploit animals."

"So what is your solution?"

"My solution is to be clear about why we cannot justify animal exploitation and why we ought to go vegan. If the person I am talking with does not care morally about animals and thinks that they are things, then that person won't go vegan. But that person is not going to reduce consumption or buy cage-free eggs either. If the person does care morally about animals and agrees with the argument but is simply not ready to go vegan, or to go vegan immediately, then that person can choose to take whatever 'baby steps' that person wants to take. But that should be their choice undertaken in the face of acknowledging that animal exploitation cannot be justified morally, and should never be what we, as animal advocates, encourage them to do."

Remember, let's give everyone as much information as possible in a free and easily accessed format on how to make the simple changes in their life that make the transition to a vegan life easy for the vast majority of people. Our website www.howdoigovegan.com is a great place to start. Show people that they don't need "baby steps."

## Sample Discussion: "It's All a Journey"

Welfarists often describe going vegan as a "journey." This sample discussion shows how that position is transparently speciesist.

> Welfarist: "The problem with you Abolitionists is that you don't recognize that going vegan is a matter of a journey. It's not something anyone is morally obligated to do immediately."
>
> Abolitionist: "But this is transparently speciesist."
>
> "How so?"
>
> "Would you ever say that people are not obligated to stop being racist and that it's a matter of a 'journey' to the rejection of racism?"
>
> "No, I wouldn't."
>
> "Alright then, why is it okay to talk about 'journeys' when we talk about animal exploitation?"
>
> "Were you born vegan?"
>
> "No, I went vegan six years ago. I was a vegetarian for five years before that."
>
> "That's exactly what I mean! See, you went on a 'journey.'"
>
> "I did not go vegan immediately. That's true. But I should have gone vegan immediately. I just did not understand the arguments in favor of going vegan. No one ever discussed the issue with me."
>
> "But if you did not go vegan immediately, how can you say other people have the obligation to go vegan immediately?"
>
> "Let me give you an example. Let's assume I grow up in a racist environment and I am a racist for the first 20 years of my life. I finally come to see that racism is wrong. Was it wrong for me to have been a racist?"
>
> "Yes."

"Should I encourage people to continue to be racists as long as they are on a 'journey' to not being racist just because I was once a racist?"

"No. You should be clear that racism is wrong."

"Exactly. So why isn't the same true of animal exploitation? If we believe that exploiting animals is morally wrong and that it violates the fundamental rights of animals, shouldn't we be clear that, even if we once violated the rights of animals, we all have a moral obligation not to violate their rights and to go vegan?"

## Sample Discussion: Single-Issue Campaigns—Eating Dogs

Welfarists support single-issue campaigns that are problematic in a number of respects, including being racist, sexist, ethnocentric, and xenophobic. In this discussion, the problems with targeting dog eating in Asia are discussed.

Welfarist: "Will you support our campaign to stop the eating of dogs in China and Korea?"

Abolitionist: "I am a vegan. I do not believe anyone should eat, wear, or use animals. But I don't support campaigns like that."

"But why? You agree that eating dogs is wrong, don't you?"

"Of course I do."

"So why won't you support the campaign?"

"In the first place, your campaign is speciesist."

"What? How can that be?"

"Your entire campaign rests on the idea that eating dogs is morally worse than eating any other sort of animal. What's the difference between eating a dog and eating a cow, chicken, pig, fish or any other animal, or eating dairy, or eating eggs?"

"There isn't. But people like dogs and they care about what happens to them."

"That's precisely the problem. Many people who eat cows, chicken, pigs, fish, or other animals, or who don't eat meat but eat dairy or eggs, support your campaign, right?"

"Yes."

"And why do they do that? They do it because they think that eating dogs is morally worse than eating these other animals—that they are better people for eating these other animals. The ones that don't eat meat but eat dairy or eggs think that dairy and eggs are morally preferable to flesh in general, but dog flesh in particular. I am not interested in supporting such a campaign that promotes the continued exploitation of other animals even if it does so implicitly."

"Well many of us are vegans."

"Yes, but you are not promoting veganism, are you? You are promoting the idea that eating dogs is wrong as some sort of isolated behavior."

"We get more support that way."

"And that is precisely the problem. Your whole campaign rests on the idea that this form of exploitation—exploitation engaged in by foreigners—is worse than other forms of exploitation that we or people we like or love engage in. The latter are seen as being morally better and not objectionable in the way that consuming dog meat is objectionable."

"Yes. But the Chinese and Koreans are really cruel and barbaric. Many of the dogs suffer prolonged deaths. They are actually butchered while still alive."

"And that brings me to my second objection to these campaigns. They are ethnocentric and xenophobic. The Chinese and Koreans are no different from anyone else. All animal slaughter is horrible. Animals killed in Western slaughterhouses all die terrible deaths and some are butchered while they are still alive. Many chickens are dropped into scalding water to facilitate the removal of their feathers while they are still alive. Campaigns like this make us think it's someone else who is engaging in the moral obscenity of victimizing the vulnerable. They are *our* moral inferiors. Sorry. No one holds a monopoly there. We are all culpable. I appreciate that you may find it easier to get donations from people if the target is the conduct done by other people—foreign people—but I won't have any part in it."

## Sample Discussion: The Anti-Fur Campaign

In this discussion, we see the speciesism and sexism of the anti-fur campaign.

Welfarist: "Are you coming to the anti-fur demonstration on Saturday?"

Abolitionist: "Absolutely not."

"Why not? Don't you think that fur is a bad thing?"

"Of course I do."

"Then why aren't you coming?"

"Because I don't see fur as any different from wearing wool, leather, or any other animal clothing. And I don't see wearing animals as any different from eating them or using them in other contexts."

"I agree but isn't it good to start somewhere?"

"I start with veganism."

"Okay. That's your approach. But what's wrong with focusing on fur as a beginning?"

"Well, for starters, it makes people think that fur is worse than leather or wool and that those sorts of animal clothing are morally better than fur. This encourages people to consume animal clothing other than fur, and that is speciesist. All forms of animal clothing involve suffering and death. Leather is skin with the hair removed; fur is skin with the hair retained. And wool involves terrible suffering, and eventual death, for sheep."

"But why can't we start with fur and then move on to those other things?"

"Because it does not work that way. If you tell people that they have to oppose fur, you explicitly or implicitly convey the idea that fur is worse than other sorts of animal clothing or other sorts of animal use. You lose your credibility if the target is always shifting. We need to be clear that any animal use is morally unjustifiable. If you can convince someone that veganism is the right thing to do, they won't wear animals. Even if you convince someone not to wear fur, that person will just buy leather or wool instead—and they will continue to eat animals and otherwise use them. Moreover, they will think that they are acting in a morally better way because the whole premise of the anti-fur campaign is that fur is worse than other sorts of animal clothing and other forms of animal exploitation. You haven't changed anything. And these campaigns simply don't work in any event. The anti-fur campaign has been around for at least fifty years and fur is more popular than it's ever been. But there is another reason not to participate in such campaigns."

"What's that?"

"This particular single-issue campaign is sexist."

"How so?"

"Most people who wear fur are women. The anti-fur campaign has always involved the expression of sexism and misogyny in various ways. Have you ever seen anyone go up to a guy wearing a leather jacket and call him the sorts of names that animal advocates regularly call women wearing fur?"

## Sample Discussion: Single-Issue Campaigns in Human and Nonhuman Contexts

Many animal advocates argue that single-issue campaigns are acceptable in the nonhuman context because we often see them in the human context. Here's an example of a discussion we have had many times with many non-Abolitionist "animal advocates."

Non-Abolitionist: "Why do you reject single-issue campaigns?"

Abolitionist: "Because they convey the idea that some forms of animal exploitation—the ones not targeted—are better than the one that is the target of the single-issue campaign. That is, when you target foie gras, or veal, you send the message that animal products other than foie gras or veal are morally better."

"But we don't say that."

"You don't have to. Your campaign includes lots of nonvegans, right? You're getting people who are not vegan contributing money and other support for your campaign, right?"

"Yes."

"Do you think that they would be supporting your campaign if they understood your position to be that what they are doing is every bit as bad as the target of your campaign?"

"But wait a minute. You could say the same thing about any single-issue campaign that involved human rights issues. You could say that we should not support efforts to assist the suffering in Haiti because we are not assisting the suffering in some other country."

"No, that's not the case. When we assist the efforts to help in Haiti, we are not making any statement that the suffering somewhere else is good. We all recognize that the suffering of innocent humans is a bad thing wherever it occurs. The fact that we choose to help in Haiti does not mean that we think that the suffering of humans in, say, Darfur, is good or that those in Darfur matter less. Similarly, the fact that we choose to work on issues of child abuse does not mean that we think rape is acceptable or is morally less objectionable. In sum, if X, Y, and Z are all viewed as morally bad, the choice to work on X does not convey the message that Y and Z are morally acceptable. A campaign against X is not going to involve the support of people who think Y and Z are good or morally better."

"Well why doesn't that apply in the animal context?"

"When it comes to animals, the analysis is different. Most people think that eating meat, dairy, and all other animal products, or wearing or using animal products, is as natural as drinking water or breathing air. So when we single out one form of animal exploitation, we necessarily distinguish it for moral purposes. That is, if we single out foie gras or veal, we convey the idea that these animal products are morally bad and that other animal products are morally better. If X, Y, and Z are all viewed as morally acceptable and you single out X as morally problematic, you implicitly say to the public that Y and Z are different from X and that they are not morally unacceptable, or are at least morally distinguishable from X. We see this problem every day: people think that fur is morally different from leather, wool, or silk; they think that meat is morally different from other animal products."

"But don't you think, if you get people to reject foie gras or veal, you can then move them further?"

"No, I think it goes the other way. If you tell someone that you want them to help you ban foie gras or veal and you explicitly or implicitly tell them that the things they are eating are morally better than foie gras or veal, and you then turn around and tell them that what they are eating is as bad as foie gras or veal, you continually move the goal post and you create the impression that you are not honest in articulating your position. This is the problem of single-issue campaigns in the context of animal exploitation. The same problem does not exist where human issues are concerned. If we campaign to help the people suffering in Haiti and then move on to the people suffering in Darfur, we are not shifting any goal posts. And we do not need single-issue campaigns in order to engage in incremental activism. There is something that each of us can do every day: be vegan and engage in creative, nonviolent vegan education."

## Sample Discussion: The "Impossibility" of Veganism

Welfarists regularly claim that we can't really be vegan in a "perfect" sense so we ought not to advocate veganism as a moral imperative. This discussion explores why that position is nonsense.

Welfarist: "You say vegans do not harm animals. But you can't avoid harming animals. Animals are killed in the process of harvesting crops."

Abolitionist: "A vegan does not participate directly and deliberately in the use of animals as human resources."

"But you can't avoid indirect and unintentional harm, such as the killing of some animals in the harvesting process."

"That's no different from the situation involving humans."

"What do you mean?"

"I buy products that are manufactured by other humans. Some humans are injured and killed in the manufacturing process. Does that mean that is the same as directly and intentionally murdering those people?"

"No."

"The same analysis holds for the nonhuman context. Growing crops will involve unintended and incidental animal deaths. And don't forget that humans are accidentally killed by farm machinery also. In any event, we ought to grow and harvest crops as carefully as possible but some animals will be killed in the process. If we did not eat animals and consumed the plants directly, we'd actually have fewer acres under cultivation so, in addition to ending animal agriculture, we would decrease the number of animals killed indirectly and unintentionally. But the point is that if it is okay for us to participate in the direct and deliberate killing of nonhumans because we cannot avoid killing them indirectly and unintentionally, then, unless you are going to take a transparently speciesist position, you have to say that it's morally acceptable to murder humans because humans are indirectly and unintentionally killed as a result of the productions of goods we all consume."

"But there are animal ingredients and by-products in everything. They are in the plastic of your computer. You can't avoid them."

"I recognize that. But that's no surprise. We kill 60 billion land animals a year. Slaughter by-products are cheap and easily available. If we stopped consuming animals, substitutes for those by-products would be developed."

"Yes, but as a vegan, how can you have a computer?"

"A vegan does not participate in animal exploitation to the extent practicable. It is not practicable not to have a computer. I also oppose racism but, when I lived in the Southern United States, I traveled on roads laid by slaves. I had no choice. That does not mean I accept slavery."

"But if you have a computer that has animal by-products in the plastic, how is that any different from eating a candy bar that has animal by-products in it?"

"It is different because one simply cannot function in modern society without devices, such as computers and phones, which are made of plastic that contains animal by-products. If you want to go to school, have a job, etc., you simply cannot avoid these things. It is entirely practicable to avoid the candy bar. If you are hungry, eat a piece of fruit instead, or wait until you get home to eat."

## A Note on Being "Divisive"

Many non-Abolitionist "animal advocates" accuse "Abolitionists" of being "divisive."

That claim makes no sense. We can only divide that which is in unity. A claim that Abolitionists are being divisive assumes that there is one movement and Abolitionists are threatening its unity.

But there isn't one movement. That's the whole point. There is the regulationist movement that rejects veganism as a moral imperative and the Abolitionist movement that has, at its very core, the principle that veganism is a matter of justice; it is a moral imperative; it is the only rational response to the position that animals are not things and matter morally.

Non-Abolitionists also claim that Abolitionists and non-Abolitionists should work together. Ask yourself this: can someone who promotes "gentle" racism work with someone who opposes racism?

\*\*\*\*\*\*\*\*\*\*

In the next chapter, we will offer some brief comments on talking with friends and family.

# Chapter 9

## Some Thoughts on Talking with Family and Friends

### Family

Sometimes, the people with whom we are closest are the most difficult people to educate about moral ideas. With families, any discussion you have about anything occurs in the context of family relationships, which often make whatever your discussion you're having more about those relationships than the topic at hand! So when you are talking with your parents about veganism, what's really going on is that you, their child, are telling your parents about how you think *their* conduct is morally wrong. And, for the most part, it's parents who see themselves in the role of being moral teachers, and not vice versa. It's not the subject that matters primarily here; it's the situation. Grandparents can sometimes be more receptive but, again, the way society is structured in most places, it is the older people who instruct the younger ones, particularly about issues of morality.

Similarly, older siblings often don't want to hear from younger siblings about anything as if they, the younger ones, "know better" than the older ones. And younger siblings resent being "lectured to" by older siblings.

So all in all, talking about moral issues with your family, and particularly anyone older than you, runs afoul of the social norm that morality is to be passed down—not educated up. Does this mean that we have to give up on family?

Absolutely not.

It does, however, mean that we need to take into consideration the family structure, the dynamics of a family as a general matter, and the dynamics of particular relationships, when we talk with our families about veganism. A good principle to observe: make it clear right from the outset that you are not saying that your family is bad morally; make it clear that you're talking about actions. Present veganism as an idea that you would like to discuss *together*. Try to place the discussion in a context that will resonate; try to find some common moral ground. Moreover, keep in mind that you are talking with people who probably think that eating animals is necessary for optimal health. This advice applies to just about any exchange, but is particularly important where families are concerned.

Here's an example:

You: "I know you don't understand my veganism, and I want to try to explain it to you. Knowing you, I really think that you'll be interested in this too. Let me preface my remarks with a caveat: I want to make it clear that I am not saying that because you are not a vegan, you are a bad person."

Family member: "What are you saying?"

"I am saying that I am a vegan because I do not believe that we can justify using animals in the ways that we do. I want to explain why I think that. But I am not saying that because you have different views that you are a bad person."

"Okay."

"Now, do you remember that, last week, you saw that news story about the man who went to Africa and shot that lion, and you said that you thought that what he did was wrong?"

"Yes."

"Why was it wrong? Why were you upset?"

"Because he killed the animal for sport."

"But he enjoyed it."

"So what?"

"Can't the enjoyment or pleasure he got out of it suffice to justify it?"

"No, of course not."

"Well now you understand a good part of why I am vegan."

"What do you mean?"

"I do not think that we can justify killing animals, or making them suffer because we get some pleasure or enjoyment out of it."

"I agree with you but how does that apply to my eating animal products? I eat meat, dairy, and eggs to stay alive—to get nutrition."

"But you don't need to do that. There is no evidence out there that you'll be less healthy if you eat a sound vegan diet. No evidence at all. As a matter of fact, most governmental and professional organizations acknowledge that. I can get you citations and you can read them for yourself. And there's also quite a bit of information out there from mainstream medical authorities that you'll be more healthy if you have a sound vegan diet."

"I'm skeptical."

"Okay, how about I get you some resources to read and you can see for yourself."

"I'll look at them."

"You see, I came to the conclusion that, if we don't need to eat animals for health, but I did so because I liked the taste, then I wasn't really different from the hunter who shoots the lion because he enjoys it."

Another way to approach a discussion with family can focus on a nonhuman animal who lives in the house and whom your parents, siblings, etc., love very much. The idea is to get them to see that there's no difference between the animals they love and the animals they eat. Again, this approach can be used in any situation.

## Friends

The same thinking applies for the most part. Friendships come with histories. You need to take those histories into account. But you also need to be clear with your friends that your veganism represents an important value for you. You should never fail to be clear about that. If someone is really your friend, then that person owes it to you to take your moral concerns seriously—whether or not they share your concerns. If someone has a sincerely held belief that, for instance, capital punishment is morally acceptable, we should be able to disagree with that position even if we disagree with it strongly and we should discuss our disagreement in a civil way that is respectful of the person.

There are three questions that we get frequently.

The first question is whether it is morally acceptable to attend events at which animal products are being served.

We do not understand how anyone can *avoid* being in the presence of animal exploitation. Even if the people at the event are not eating any animal products, they are, most likely, wearing wool or leather. There is no difference between eating animals and wearing animals. If you will attend an event with, or be in the presence of someone who is wearing wool or leather, what's the difference between that and being at an event where animal products are being served? An Abolitionist does not compromise their moral beliefs by attending such events. Indeed, we do not know how it is possible to avoid those events! We do, however, think that you should always take every opportunity you have to educate people about veganism. Places where people are engaged in nonvegan behavior are good places to find potential vegans to educate!

The second question is whether, when you are out with friends, you should ask the server or chef questions to make sure that the food you order is vegan. Our answer is, "Yes, of course."

The reason why we are asked this is that some "animal advocates" have argued that you harm animals if you make veganism look too difficult. People who share this view maintain that you should not ask servers in restaurants about ingredients, and should not send something back if it comes with animal ingredients.

We could not disagree more. If you are in a restaurant that serves animal products and you don't inquire in situations where it's not clear that what you're ordering is vegan, or you don't send back the pasta when it comes sprinkled with cheese or meat bits, then you've made a very clear statement to your friends: you don't take veganism seriously. You've told them by your actions that veganism is not a moral imperative as far as you are concerned.

The third question is whether we think it's morally acceptable to have close relationships (including sexual relationships) with people who are not vegans.

We are not relationship counselors. Our view here is that we should endeavor to educate *everyone*. If you have a close friendship or a sexual relationship with someone who, after you make a concerted effort to educate, has nothing to say in defense of their animal exploitation, and who continues to participate directly in animal exploitation, you need to make a decision as to whether you want to continue that relationship. We're not going to say more because each situation will differ and there may be complicating facts, such as the presence of children in a relationship, that make situations unique and may make acceptable solutions difficult to reach.

We do, however, want to make one thing clear: you should never be ashamed of loving someone who is not vegan. It is not immoral to love or live with a nonvegan. What is immoral is compromising your position on fundamental rights—of humans or nonhumans—to please or accommodate another person. For example, consuming animal products in order to accommodate a partner, parent, or friend is no different from participating in a violation of fundamental human rights in order to accommodate that person.

## A Note About Children and Their Peers

A question we get a fair amount involves how to help vegan children deal with their peers, who can often be merciless in their ridicule of veganism.

Unfortunately, children often ridicule other children for any number of reasons, including, their beliefs. Children are often confronted with having to decide whether they are going to adhere to their beliefs or abandon them so that they can fit in. This makes it all the more important that they understand Abolitionist veganism as a principle of justice and that it is firmly developed as one of their core beliefs. This will help them to get through any period of taunting or bullying just as a clear understanding and acceptance of civil rights would militate against their participating in racist behavior.

You should make sure to talk with your vegan child's teachers to make sure that your child's beliefs are accommodated so that they can fully participate in and enjoy school trips and celebrations.

\*\*\*\*\*\*\*\*\*\*

In the next chapter, we talk about how to deal with someone who wants to go vegan but is very anxious.

# Chapter 10

## Dealing with Anxiety About Veganism

There are people who really do want to go vegan but who find the idea *intimidating*.

This is not all that surprising.

Many people become anxious at the thought of having to drive a different route to go to work or to make other changes in their lives that are trivial. So the idea of no longer eating, wearing, or using animal products may produce palpable anxiety for some people.

For most people, exploiting animals is something that they have done all of their lives and they haven't given it much, if any, thought. In proposing that they go vegan, you are asking them to consider no longer doing something that they have, up to this point, regarded as normal as breathing or drinking water.

Moreover, if the person has been involved with animal organizations in the past, you can be certain that they've been exposed to all the propaganda about how difficult it is to go vegan.

So however easy you think it is to go vegan, and however easy your transition was, it is imperative that you take seriously expressions of anxiety or concern in this context.

Here are some simple suggestions.

*First,* always emphasize that going vegan is easy. It is easy for nearly everyone. All of this nonsense from the large animal groups about how difficult it is to go vegan is just that—nonsense.

*Second,* focus on the fact that going vegan, at least as far as food is concerned, does not really involve a qualitative change; it's more a quantitative change. The person is already eating fruits, vegetables, grains, beans, and seeds/nuts. The problem is that she is also eating meat, fish, dairy, eggs, and honey. The idea is to emphasize that she is almost vegan already; she just needs to increase the amounts of the other foods that she is already eating, and eliminate the animal products. This presents the issue in a much less intimidating way. Let's ditch once and for all the idea that veganism requires eating expensive foods, cooking all day, grinding your own flour, etc. Eating vegan is not a full-time job!

*Third,* be prepared to refer the person to sources where they can learn about nutrition and read about what government and medical authorities say about a vegan diet—that a sound vegan diet can provide for optimal health and may have health benefits over a diet that contains animal products. Emphasize that they can learn everything they need to learn about vegan sources of B-12, iron, zinc, calcium, and protein in about an hour. We created our website, www.howdoigovegan.com, precisely to serve this purpose.

*Fourth,* be prepared to be able to provide some easy recipes or point the person to websites that have easy and cheap vegan recipes. Again, our website provides recipes but there are an endless number of sites available that provide information on every sort of possible food choice: raw, cooked, low fat, gluten-free, Indian, Spanish, Italian, Turkish, etc. Getting all the recipe information you need is as easy as having access to the internet, or to a local library.

## Alleviating Anxiety: A Sample Discussion

Here is an example of a conversation we had with a woman after a recent speaking event:

Woman: "That was a terrific talk. Thank you so much. You've convinced me! I want to go vegan."

Us: "That's great."

"I have to say that I find it a bit overwhelming. I can't do it straightaway."

"Of course you can. Why do you think you can't?"

"I don't know where to start. It's hard."

"Okay. Why do you say that?"

"Well, to start off, I don't know what to eat."

"What is your diet now?"

"I don't eat any red meat. I do eat chicken occasionally. I eat fish mostly. I do eat some cheese. I drink milk. I don't eat eggs much but I will eat them if they are used to make other foods, like cake."

"Do you eat vegetables?"

"Sure. I love them."

"How about fruits?"

"Yes. I love them, too."

"Do you like grains?"

"Sure. I usually have short-grain brown rice in the refrigerator. I make a big pot every few days."

"That's terrific. How do you feel about beans?"

"I eat a lot of navy and cannellini beans."

"Do you like nuts and seeds?"

"Yes, I just bought pumpkin seeds yesterday."

"That's great. Pumpkin seeds are really good for you. They're loaded with zinc."

"Yes, I know."

"Okay. You're already 80% there. All you need to do is eat more of the foods you are already eating and stop eating all the stuff that violates the rights of animals."

Note here what we are doing: we are focusing on both the ease of a vegan diet and the fact that it will *not* represent a significant departure from where she already is. The idea is to make a vegan diet both less difficult and less strange; the goal is to try to decrease anxiety. So we present veganism, at least as far as food is concerned, as not involving some seismic shift—it is just a matter of increasing the quantities of things that people are already eating and eliminating some of the other things they are eating.

Let's return to the discussion:

Woman: "But what about nutrition?"

Us: "There's really not much to learn. We have a website, www.howdoigovegan.com, which tells you about things like vitamin B-12, iron, zinc, calcium, protein, etc. You can learn everything you need to learn in about an hour. And don't worry. We're not health care practitioners but if you read the sites we refer you to, you'll see you can get *everything* you need to be healthy from plants. This website also provides all the governmental and professional sites that reinforce the adequacy of a vegan diet."

"I am not a great cook!"

"You don't have to be. There are tons of really easy recipes that anyone can do. Whatever you want, whatever nationality of cuisine, gluten-free, raw, cooked, low-fat, whatever."

"It's that easy?"

"It's easier than easy!"

"Can you give me some sites to get me started?"

"On our website, we have tons of information. Use that as a

one-stop resource. And if you have questions, we have vegans available through the website who can provide answers and mentoring."

"That's great. Is it expensive to be vegan?"

"Prepared vegan foods that you buy in upscale markets can be pricey. But they're loaded with salt and have little nutritional value. But fruits, vegetables, grains, beans, seeds, are not expensive at all. It's much cheaper to eat as a vegan. On our website, we have many recipes that cost only a few cents per portion."

"Organic produce is expensive, right?"

"Organic produce is often more expensive and can be more expensive than the non-organic animal products you may eat, but the comparison is not between organic produce and non-organic meat. It's between non-organic meat and non-organic produce, which will almost always be cheaper."

"Thanks, much. I will take a look at the website!"

We received an email from this person a few weeks later. She had stopped eating all animal products and asked where she could get vegan clothing and shoes!

## The Really Hard Cases

On a number of occasions, we have encountered people who, after extended discussion, respond by saying that they are just too anxious to go vegan immediately. They want to know what they can do as an interim matter in order to ease into being vegan.

We always respond the same way: if they agree that animal exploitation is wrong and violates the fundamental rights of animals, then they have, in essence, acknowledged that they have an obligation to act on that recognition and to go vegan.

It's that simple. If they recognize that it is wrong and violates the fundamental rights of beings who have moral value, then there really isn't much more to say.

But what happens if they revert and say, "yes, I understand that, but

I just can't do it. How can I ease into it rather than just make a dramatic change that causes me a great deal of anxiety?"

In such circumstances, as a last resort, we have used what we call the "three-step strategy." This involves removing all animal products from breakfast for a week. And then remove all animal products from lunch for a week. And then do dinner.

We have had tremendous success with this over the years but we are always clear: animal exploitation is morally unjustifiable and this is even more serious when a person recognizes that animal exploitation involves a violation of the fundamental rights of animals. It is imperative that you make clear that it is wrong to continue consuming animal products and that you are not in *any* way putting a stamp of approval on this conduct.

Here is a sample discussion, which is based on a conversation we had with a student:

Student: "I agree completely with the arguments you've made. I want to go vegan. I do."

Us: "That's great."

"But I'm a bit anxious."

"About what?"

"It's a big change."

"Not really. It's just eating more of what you already eat and are familiar with, and eliminating some of the other stuff."

"Yeah, I get that. But I still am overwhelmed by the idea."

"You agree it's wrong to exploit animals, right?"

"Absolutely. I have bought into the arguments totally."

"Well, then, you understand you have a moral obligation."

"Yes, I do."

"So why not just act on it?"

"Because the idea freaks me out. Isn't there any way to ease into it?"

"No more so than with any other fundamental rights violation. Once you recognize that something violates the fundamental rights of others, you stop. Period."

"Yes, but I have spent my whole life eating animal foods."

"So have most people."

"Look, I can't do it cold turkey. Oops. Sorry for the turkey reference!"

"Sure you can."

"Really, I am telling you I can't. Can you suggest anything?"

"Well, you can remove the animal products completely from breakfast for a week. You will see that you don't die and your arms and legs don't fall off. You can then do all-plants for lunch for a week, and then all-plants for dinner. Then you have a vegan diet."

"That sounds do-able. I am going to try that. Thanks so much."

"Let's be clear on something. We're not saying that it's okay for you or anyone to do this. There's no stamp of approval here. That's the whole thing about veganism being a moral imperative. It's a moral obligation. Every animal product you eat involves a violation of that obligation. We're not saying that it's okay as far as morality is concerned. It's not okay. We think you should just stop doing what *you've* acknowledged is wrong. But if this is the only thing you feel you can do then do it with your moral eyes open!"

"I understand."

This student came to class several weeks later and said that he had eased into a totally plant-based diet and that it was the easiest thing he had ever done. We both said—at the exact same time—"told you so!"

There are some people who claim that this "three-step" approach is similar to the "journey" or "baby steps" promoted by the non-Abolitionist "animal advocates." That involves what can only be a willful misrepresentation—or a profound misunderstanding—of what we're saying. Non-Abolitionists promote "baby steps," such as cage-free eggs, crate-free pork, "happy milk," Meatless Monday, reducetarianism, etc. as *good* things. They do not promote veganism as a moral baseline. They promote it as a way of reducing suffering (to the extent that they promote it at all). For non-Abolitionists, animal use per se is not presented as violating the fundamental rights of animals—it is only the suffering that is the problem. They promote "baby steps" as good things; as things that people *ought* to do.

We do not promote the "three-step" strategy as morally good or as something that anyone ought to do. We offer it only as a practical response to the irrational fear that some people have about going vegan. We never put a stamp of approval on *any* animal exploitation, and, if you are an Abolitionist, neither should you.

\*\*\*\*\*\*\*\*\*

In the next chapter, we consider how to advocate when faced with objections to Abolitionist veganism by "animal advocates" who reject Abolition.

# Chapter 11

## Seven Common Objections to Veganism: Sample Discussions

In *Eat Like You Care: An Examination of the Morality of Eating Animals*, we examined approximately 36 common objections to veganism. We refer you to that book as we don't think that there are many common objections that we didn't cover.

In this chapter, we are going to pick six of those objections but, rather than repeating what we said in our earlier book, we are going to place them in the context of actual discussions so you can see how these objections can be addressed in concrete contexts. Every discussion you have will be different but you will at least get an idea about how to approach these issues. In addition, we will consider one objection we did not discuss in *Eat Like You Care*: that morality is just a matter of opinion.

### Plants

If you are doing vegan advocacy and you don't have someone ask you about why it's not morally acceptable to eat animals but it is morally acceptable to eat plants, then consider yourself *very* fortunate. In the 30+ years that we have been doing vegan advocacy, we have gotten the "plant" question literally *thousands* of times.

For the most part, the discussions follow a similar pattern. The person asking about plants is trying to get you to see that there is no morally important difference between eating plants and eating animals because, in both cases, a *living* being is killed. Your task is to explain that being alive is not the same thing as being *sentient*. Here goes:

Plant advocate: "You say that we shouldn't eat animals but you eat plants."

Abolitionist: "That's right on both counts. I do say that it's wrong to eat animals and I do eat plants."

"Isn't that hypocritical?"

"How so?"

"Well, plants are alive too."

"That's true. But they're not sentient."

"What do you mean by 'sentience'?"

"To be sentient is to be subjectively aware; that is, there is some sort of mind—however simple—that is aware of things; there is some sort of mind that has interests; that is, has preferences, desires, or wants of some sort."

"How do you know that plants are not sentient?"

"Do you think that plants are subjectively aware in any sense?"

"Well, they're alive."

"Of course they are. That's not the issue. The issue is whether they are sentient."

"They act in very complicated ways."

"Yes, they do, but so do the cells of your body. Are your cells sentient?"

"When they are threatened, plants react in defensive ways."

"Some may but so do cancer tumors. Are they sentient? The question is whether plants, cells, tumors and the like have interests. That is, do they have preferences, desires, or wants? I think the answer is clearly, 'no.'"

"Plants have an interest in being watered."

"That is a metaphorical use of 'interest.' It is no different from saying that a car engine has an 'interest' in being oiled. Just as the car engine has no sort of mind that prefers, wants, or desires anything, so, too, the plant has no sort of mind that prefers, wants, or desires anything. Plants cannot have interests."

"But aren't you doing exactly what you accuse others of doing? You say that cognitive differences don't matter and an elephant and a chicken are equal in terms of their moral value, but you now seem to be saying that a plant is less morally valuable than an animal."

"I am not saying that plants matter less than animals because they are less sophisticated cognitively. I am saying that plants don't matter morally *at all* because they are not sentient. Nothing I can do to a plant can adversely affect the plant. That is, I cannot in any way cause distress or pain to a plant. There is no one there who has any interests that I can frustrate."

"But there is scientific evidence that plants are sentient."

"No, that's not true. There is no scientific evidence that plants are sentient. None. There is a great deal of evidence that plants behave in all sorts of complex ways. I don't dispute that. As I said to you before, individual cells and tumors do all sorts of complex things. There is no scientific evidence that plants have any sort of mind whatsoever. When newspapers run sensationalist stories about plants having 'feelings,' if you look at the actual research they are relying on, there is never any claim that plants have any sort of mind that prefers, wants, or desires anything."

"Plants might be sentient."

"What is that supposed to mean? All sorts of things that are not the case *might* be the case. The point is that there is no evidence that plants have any sort of mind that prefers, wants, or desires anything. Moreover, why would plants evolve anything beyond the reactions that they have? Why would they develop any sort of mind that was subjectively aware given that their being sentient would in no way assist them to survive?"

"How do you draw the line between sentient and non-sentient?"

"It's not a problem with 99.99% of the animals we exploit. There is no doubt that all the cows, turkeys, fish, sheep, pigs, and chickens are sentient. There may be some doubt on bivalves such as clams and oysters. We err in favor of their being sentient and we don't eat them. Similarly, there is doubt as to whether insects are sentient. There is some indication they are and some indication they are not. So we err in favor of not deliberately killing them."

"Let me ask you hypothetically, what would you do if you found that plants were sentient?"

"There would be two choices. The first choice would be to stop eating plants as well as animals and just starve to death. The second choice would be to decide to live and to eat plants. If plants are sentient and we consume them directly, we will still end up killing *many* fewer plants than we do by growing plants and then feeding many pounds of plants to animals for every one pound of animal products that we get back. In other words, even if plants were sentient, which they are not, we should still be eating plants if we decide not to commit suicide."

"So you don't think that plants scream when you pick them or eat them?"

"No, and neither do you! If I chopped up a head of lettuce in front of you, you would react very differently from the way you would if I chopped up a live chicken! It seems that no one ever thinks that plants are sentient until the issue of exploiting sentient animals is raised."

## Tradition

It is common for people to argue against veganism on the ground that eating animals and animal products is traditional, either as a general matter or in connection with particular cultural traditions. This is an easy point to rebut.

Traditionalist: "You say we should be vegan but eating animals is traditional; we've been doing it forever."

Abolitionist: "So what? What is the moral relevance of the fact that we've been doing something for a long time? We've been sexist for a long time. We've been racist for a long time. We've waged wars for a long time. We've harmed children in all sorts of ways for a long time. The fact that we've been doing something for a long time does not in any way translate into any sort of moral value."

"But what about the fact that eating animal foods is so much a part of particular cultures?"

"Food and other animal uses are central to just about all cultures. The same analysis holds. Everything in the world that is wrong is part of someone's culture. The fact that something is part of a cultural tradition does not say *anything* about its morality. Think about it this way—female genital mutilation is a tradition in some cultures. Does that make it morally acceptable?"

"But isn't it wrong to criticize the cultures of others?"

"No, not unless you are a cultural relativist who thinks that right and wrong are determined by cultural values. I am not a cultural relativist. I do not believe that we have any obligation to not speak out against injustice because injustice is part of someone's culture."

## The Food Chain

A standard objection to veganism is that it is morally acceptable for humans to exploit animals because humans are at the top of the "food chain." This is shorthand way of saying that humans are "superior" to animals, which, in turn, is a shorthand way of saying that humans are super predators who are capable of exploiting and oppressing all other species. That may be true but, just as in the case of the "tradition" argument, it carries *no* moral weight whatsoever.

Food chain advocate: "I eat animals because we humans are at the top of the food chain."

Abolitionist: "What 'chain' are you speaking of? Are you saying that there is a real chain that places us at the top?"

"No, not a real chain but we are the most powerful predator on earth."

"And that means that we have the right to exploit and oppress other animals?"

"It's a sort of natural order."

"So if the United States is more powerful than other nations, then it is 'natural,' and therefore right, that the United States exploit and oppress others?"

"No, I wasn't saying that."

"But the 'food chain' argument seems to say that what is morally right is that which accommodates the interests of the powerful."

"I was saying more that nature is configured such that we are at the top."

"But don't you see that you're just *assuming* that it's alright to exploit animals? There is no real 'top' or 'bottom' because there isn't any 'chain.' The argument you are making is that it is morally acceptable to exploit animals because we can exploit animals. That is no different from saying that it is morally acceptable for stronger humans to exploit weaker humans because they can."

## Choice

We tend to think of choice as a good thing. We like that we are able to choose to do things. But the fact that we can choose to do something does not make it right. We frequently hear things like the following:

Choice advocate: "I am tired of you vegans imposing your views."

Abolitionist: "How am I imposing my views? We are discussing an issue and I have given you my position. I am happy to hear yours."

"Well, it's my choice to eat animal products or to wear leather or wool or whatever."

"I do not in any way challenge the fact that you *can* choose to exploit animals. It's not illegal to do so. The issue is whether you *should* make that choice. I can choose to treat you in a callous, rude, or unfair way. Should I do so?"

"No."

"Well, then, the fact that you can choose to eat meat or drink milk or wear leather—the fact that the law does not prohibit you from doing those things—is not the question. The question is whether you *should* choose to do any of those things."

In this situation, it is important to argue that we have choices among options that are morally acceptable. We choose options that give us pleasure, sustenance, or are convenient from among a range of morally acceptable options. But, as a moral matter, we can only choose from among those acceptable options. We do not have the right to choose to inflict pain, suffering, and death on another sentient being, so animal foods are not among the range of acceptable options.

We can choose *what* to eat, not *whom* to eat.

## The Desert Island

We never realized how many lone individuals must be stranded on desert islands until we started vegan advocacy!

*Every* vegan has been asked about what they would do if they were on a desert island. Would they then eat animals? The idea here is that if vegans would not be vegans if their lives depended on it, then veganism cannot really be a moral imperative. Let's see how the discussion unfolds:

Desert island advocate: "So you think veganism is a moral obligation—it is something we all are required to do?"

Abolitionist: "Yes."

"Okay, so if you were on a desert island and there was nothing else to eat except an animal, you would starve to death?"

"First of all, why are we talking about desert islands? Have you or has anyone you know ever been starving on a desert island or on a lifeboat?"

"No, but I want to try to understand better what your position is, so can you please tell me: in such a situation, would you starve?"

"Probably not."

"What? Then you cannot believe that animals have rights."

"That's not true at all."

"Can you explain that to me because I think your being willing to eat the animal means that it cannot be a moral obligation not to eat animals."

"We have to distinguish between *moral justification* and *moral excuse*. If we say that an action is morally justified, that means that it's a morally acceptable thing—a good thing—to do. If we say that action is excusable, that means that it is morally wrong but its wrongness is mitigated, or lessened, by the circumstances, which usually involve a compulsion that effectively takes away a person's choice."

"Can you give me an example?"

"Sure. If a person is about to kill me for no reason and I defend myself and kill that person, I have acted in a morally justifiable way. What I did was morally right. There's a *justification* for what I did. I did nothing wrong."

"Okay. Yes, I see that."

"But let's assume that you put a gun to my child's head and say that if I do not rob a store, you will kill my child. Assume that there is nothing I can do to save my child's life except to rob the store. That is, I can't go to the police or do anything to save my child other than to rob the store. In that situation, there is compulsion. I can't really choose not to rob the store. But robbing the store is wrong. The store owner is innocent. So if I rob the store, I have done something wrong but the wrongness of my act is mitigated, or lessened, by the fact that I didn't really have any choice. My action is not justified but it may be *excused*. Do you understand the distinction I am making?"

"Yes."

"Okay. If I am on a desert island and I am starving to death, then there is clearly a compulsion there that gets in the way of my making a moral choice, right?"

"Yes."

"In such circumstances, humans have been known to kill and eat *other humans*. And the law has sometimes been forgiving in such circumstances precisely because, although it is recognized that killing and eating someone is wrong, the compulsion in such a situation lessens the blameworthiness. But even in those situations, no one says that it is a morally good thing to kill and eat someone. It is wrong. But it is a wrong that happens in a context of compulsion so it's a great deal less wrong than a wrong that happened as a result of choice. The same thing applies where animals are involved. If I am on a desert island and there are no plants to eat, and I kill and eat an animal, that's morally wrong but the moral wrongness must be evaluated in the context of the compulsion of the situation. It's rather hard to make a moral choice when the options are only to live or die. So my eating the animal is wrong precisely because I have an obligation not to exploit animals. But my wrong action may be excused because I really had no other choice."

"So you would not treat the human and nonhuman situations differently?"

"No, in both cases, we are treating another exclusively as a means to our ends. That is wrong. It is equally wrong because the human and the nonhuman are equal in terms of their right not to be treated as means to our ends. But we must keep one thing firmly in mind here: when you are deciding what to eat tonight for dinner or what sort of shoes you should buy, there is no compulsion. There is nothing remotely like the desert island scenario. There is no conflict at all. And that brings me back to my original point: you are not on a desert island starving. You are here, now, and your choice to consume animal products cannot in any way be regarded as justifiable *or* excusable."

# God

We have all encountered situations in which someone says that animal exploitation is authorized by God. That is, they maintain that you can't be correct that it is morally wrong to exploit animals because their religion maintains that God says that animal exploitation is just fine. Keeping in mind that religious people can be very difficult to educate if they are unwilling to engage any rational argument, there are at least two responses you can offer *if* the person is willing to engage you.

*First,* you show the person that they don't really think that whatever their sacred scriptures say defines morality. Almost all religions have a God who makes all sorts of pronouncements and who authorizes all sorts of things with which no one would agree, so this approach would apply in almost all conversations. For example, the Old Testament, which is the basis of the Christian and Jewish traditions, has God seemingly approving all sorts of things that not even a fundamentalist would agree with, such as slavery and rape. Both the Old Testament and the New Testament say that women should not speak at a religious service. Most religious people think that slavery and rape are morally wrong, and that it is also morally wrong to take the position that women should be prohibited from speaking in a religious service. But how could that be if the religious texts define morality?

The answer is simple: anyone who says that they are a Christian or religious Jew and that they reject slavery, rape, and prohibiting women from speaking at religious services is *necessarily* using a standard of right and wrong that is separate from what God or the Bible says is morally acceptable. That is, they cannot simultaneously say that what is morally right or wrong is found in the revealed word of God in the Bible, but that they reject some of that because it is morally wrong without there being a moral standard *separate* from God that they are using to decide what they do agree and don't agree with.

So the first thing to focus on is why, given everything else in the Old Testament that no one would ever think is morally acceptable, does anyone assume that what God apparently says about animals is something that cannot be analyzed morally? If you are going to reject rape as immoral despite the fact that God has Lot, one of the good guys of the Bible, offering his daughters to be raped to satisfy the sexual urges of angry neighbors (Genesis 19:1-8), why do you not object to what you regard as God saying it's morally acceptable to exploit animals?

Try to get the person to see that, despite saying that religion defines what is moral, they are using a moral standard that is separate and apart from what God says. If the person really believed that God defines morality, they would have no problem in concluding that what Lot did was just fine and that we, too, should feel free to exploit women and treat them violently when it is convenient. The issue is whether you can get them to see that, and that they should, in a similar way, think critically about what a religious text or tradition says about animal exploitation.

*Second,* you can point out that the religious texts that are usually used to justify animal exploitation often do not say what they are thought to say, or are open to a very different interpretation. Again, take the Old Testament. In Genesis, the first book, we are told that God gave humans "dominion" over animals. This is interpreted by many as saying that God said that animal exploitation is just fine. But it's more complicated than that. As we explained in *Eat Like You Care*, the first chapter of Genesis has God creating the world, including humans and nonhumans, and telling *everyone* that they should eat the herb and the seed (Genesis 1:29-30). There is no killing, of humans by humans, of humans by animals, animals by humans, or animals by other animals. Killing only begins after humans break the covenant with God by disobeying God and eating the fruit from the forbidden tree. Humans enter a "fallen" state where death is possible and they begin to kill each other. It is only then that God allows humans to kill animals for food—arguably as an accommodation to the fallen state of humans.

But it is also clear later in the Old Testament that the ideal situation that will come about after the covenant is restored, will return to a situation where we won't kill anymore, and there will be peace between humans, who will "beat their swords into ploughshares, and their spears into pruninghooks: nation shall not lift up sword against nation, neither shall they learn war any more." (Isaiah 2:4) And peace will also extend to and amongst nonhumans: "The wolf and the lamb shall feed together, and the lion shall eat straw like the bullock: and dust shall be the serpent's meat. They shall not hurt nor destroy in all my holy mountain, saith the Lord." (Isaiah 65:25).

So a very good argument could be made that not exploiting animals is what religious people should aspire to.

Let's see how this plays out in an actual conversation we had with an acquaintance who is a somewhat devout Christian:

Devout person: "I hear what you are saying but your moral framework is not my moral framework. For me, morality is a matter of God's word."

Abolitionist: "Okay, and you think that if God says you don't have to be a vegan, then an argument that we have a moral obligation to be vegan can't be a good argument?"

"Exactly."

"So what is morally required is what God says you ought to do?"

"Yes, if it is a subject or matter that has been discussed in the Bible."

"So what is morally right or wrong is that which God commands or allows?"

"Yes."

"So if God appears to you and tells you to kill your child, as God did to Abraham, that means it's morally acceptable—indeed, morally obligatory—to do so."

"God stopped Abraham from killing his son."

"Yes, but Abraham was prepared to kill his son had God not stopped him."

"I believe God would never ask us to do anything wrong."

"But that suggests that there's a standard of right and wrong apart from God? If you say that it's wrong to kill your child and that's why God would not ask you to do it, then that necessarily means that God doesn't define right or wrong."

"Yes, I suppose it does. I need to think about that."

"But let me ask you as a general matter, the Bible has all sorts of things in it. In the Old Testament, for example, there is a great deal of violence that God commands or allows. Do you think that, for example, it was morally acceptable for Lot to offer his daughters to be raped by his neighbors?"

"No, of course not."

"The Bible says that woman should not speak in a religious service. Do you agree with that?"

"No."

"But if the Bible is the revealed word of God, then how can you pick and choose? You must have some standard that is separate and apart from God that helps you to determine what you think is obligatory and what you think is not obligatory and may even be morally very wrong, such as rape, or slavery."

"I can see what you are saying. But it is very clear in Genesis that God gives dominion to humans over animals. I can't see how that could be more clear."

"What is clear is that everyone was vegan in the beginning."

"What are you talking about?"

"Well, it's your Bible; you should read it!"

"I have."

"Well, in Genesis, God says to humans: 'I have given you every herb bearing seed, which is upon the face of all the earth, and every tree, in the which is the fruit of a tree yielding seed; to you it shall be for meat.' And then God told all the animals and birds, 'I have given every green herb for meat: and it was so.' That's at Genesis, chapter 1, verses 29-30. Killing does not begin until after Adam and Eve eat the fruit from the forbidden tree and are expelled from the garden."

"But whatever happened at the beginning, God certainly allows humans to eat animals."

"Yes, God permits it but apparently as an accommodation to the fallen state of humans. But the original situation remains the ideal. When the prophet Isaiah talks about the coming of the Messiah and the re-establishment of God's kingdom on earth, how does he describe it? First, there will be peace between humans, who will 'beat their swords into ploughshares, and their spears into pruninghooks: nation shall not lift up sword against nation, neither shall they learn war any more.' That's at Isaiah, chapter 2, verse 4. Second, peace will also extend to and amongst nonhumans: 'The wolf and the lamb shall feed together, and the lion shall eat straw like the bullock: and dust shall be the serpent's meat. They shall not hurt nor destroy in all my holy mountain, saith the Lord.' That's at Isaiah, chapter 65, verse 25."

"You have an interesting take on all this. I never really thought about it this way."

"Don't you think that, if you care about being spiritual, it's better to aspire to the more spiritually enlightened state?"

"Yes, but what about the fact that Jesus divided loaves and fishes so he could not have been a vegan?"

"First of all, the four Gospels that were included in the New Testament were written a long time after the historical figure Jesus existed so it is not clear how historically accurate they are. Second, there are some who believe, based on the discovery of the Dead Sea Scrolls, that Jesus was an Essene. Essenes did not consume animal foods. But even if you reject that, and even if you believe that Jesus ate fish, are you saying that God *requires* you to consume animal products?"

"No, but I am allowed to not be a vegan. And why would I choose veganism when Jesus did not choose veganism?"

"I appreciate your belief in the divinity of Jesus but surely you cannot think that the biblical account of his life addresses all moral issues. After all, he lived at a particular time. Does that account address all of the problems that would develop in the Middle East? Does Jesus address all of the moral issues concerning the role of women in society in the way that we now are? I am not sure how much we can infer from his eating fish if, in fact, he ate fish."

"Yes, I can see what you are saying."

"So if you engage in a moral analysis of animal exploitation—just as you did in determining what in the Old Testament you would and would not observe—and you conclude that exploiting animals is morally wrong, nothing requires that you continue to exploit animals, does it?"

"No, of course not."

"Then maybe you ought to think about that moral analysis and see whether you think that we can justify animal exploitation."

"I will."

We can report that this particular person went vegan about two months after our conversation. He told us that what really had an impact on him was that he had not, until our conversation, realized that although he said that he thought all morality came from God's commands, he was using a moral standard separate and apart from God to determine that which he regarded as obligatory and that which he did not. He decided that the exploitation of animals could not be morally justified.

We are not theologians and we would not deny that there are all sorts of statements in most religions that support the idea that humans are given some sort of divine "permission" to consume animals. But we would return to the simple and indisputable fact that no one—not the most fundamentalist person—follows the scriptures of her or his religion to the precise letter. Everyone uses some *other* moral standard—other than what is in religious texts—to determine what to do or not to do.

Moreover, we would point out that most religious scriptures were written at a time in history when people really could not—for various reasons—conceive of not eating or using animals for human needs. They may have thought that eating animal foods was necessary for existence or that animals had to be killed to provide clothing. But that is no longer the case.

Most of the world's religions explicitly endorse the idea that animals have some moral value. To inflict suffering and death on animals for no reason other than palate pleasure or fashion sense cannot be made consistent with those religious traditions.

## Morality

In the previous section, we dealt with the person who thinks that morality is a matter of what God or religion says. But what about the person who says that morality is a matter of opinion?

When we encounter such a person, the first question we ask is: "So you are saying the morality of the Holocaust is a matter of opinion. If your opinion is that there was nothing wrong with the Holocaust, then that ends the matter? There is nothing more to say?"

No one ever responds, "Yes, the morality of killing of millions of innocent people, including Jews, Poles, and Romanies, for no reason other than a mentally-deranged desire to rid the world of non-Ayrans, is simply a matter of opinion." No one *says* that; no one *believes* that.

The fact is that just about no one really believes that morality is simply a matter of opinion until you are talking with them about how they have an obligation to go vegan! Then, all of a sudden, morality becomes nothing more than a matter of opinion. People may have different reasons for believing that morality is not simply a matter of opinion and, in some cases, they may have no reason at all, at least one that they can articulate. The reason why most people think that the morality of the Holocaust is not a matter of opinion is because the Holocaust violated a moral principle that most see as *self-evidently true*: that it is morally wrong to torture and kill innocent humans.

But most of us also accept as self-evidently true the principle that it is wrong to make animals suffer or to kill animals without a good reason. We have never met anyone—including people who exploit animals in all sorts of ways—who disagrees with the principle that it is morally wrong to inflict unnecessary suffering on animals. Again, most people may not have an articulable reason as to why they accept this moral principle as true, but they do see it as self-evidently true.

The differences in particular positions concern the different views that people have about what is "necessary." Every animal exploiter we have encountered believes that whatever it is they are doing or supporting is necessary. For example, most people who eat animals or animal products think that consuming animals is necessary for optimal health. Most people who engage in hunting animals not only believe that eating animals is necessary for human health but that hunting is necessary to ensure ecological balance. Those who use animals in biomedical research believe that it is necessary to use animals to get data that they need. Even those who support animal exploitation in the context of entertainment consider that there is some element of necessity involved. For example, those who support bullfighting claim that it is necessary as part of the preservation of Spanish culture. Those who support rodeos claim that they are necessary as a part of the preservation of American culture.

For the most part, debates about animal use focus on whether the purported "necessity" claims are valid or not. But the starting point for all these disputes is the principle that imposing suffering on animals requires *some* justification.

So when someone with whom you are talking about veganism says that it's all a matter of opinion, ask them a simple question: do you agree that it's morally wrong to impose unnecessary suffering on animals? If the person says that they do not agree and that it's perfectly fine to impose gratuitous suffering on animals, then go on and talk with someone else because you won't get anywhere with someone who really believes that.

But, as we have said, there are few people who take that position. The overwhelming number of people agree that we shouldn't impose unnecessary suffering on animals. Your job is to educate them about how eating, wearing, and otherwise using animals are not in any way necessary.

Let's run through a very typical discussion that involves these ideas:

Relativist: "Well, if you want to be a vegan, that's your choice. But it's my choice not to be a vegan."

Abolitionist: "Sure, you can choose to not be vegan. The issue is whether it is immoral not to be a vegan."

"Yes, but who says what is moral? It's a matter of individual opinion."

"So you think morality is a matter of opinion?"

"Yes, I do."

"So the moral status of the Holocaust is a matter of opinion? One of us can think it morally right and the other think it morally wrong and there's no truth of the matter?"

"I wouldn't say that. We all agree that the Holocaust was wrong."

"Yes, we do, or most of us at least. And why do we think that?"

"Because the victims were all innocent people."

"And so?"

"It's wrong to kill innocent people."

"And that's true?"

"Yes."

"How do you know it's true?"

"I never really thought about it. I would say it is self-evident—you shouldn't kill innocent people."

"So morality is not simply a matter of opinion?"

"Not on that level."

"Okay, do you think that animals matter at all morally?"

"What do you mean?"

"Well, does anything we do to or with animals raise a moral issue? If someone tortures a dog for no reason other than to derive pleasure, does that raise a moral issue at all?"

"Sure."

"Why?"

"Because there is no reason to torture the dog."

"Well, there *is* a reason—to derive pleasure."

"But that is sick."

"Why is it sick?"

"For the same reason that killing innocent people is wrong. It is self-evident. Only a psychopath would disagree."

"So would you say that you think that the principle that it's wrong to impose gratuitous or unnecessary suffering on an animal is a principle that is similar to the principle that it is wrong to kill innocent humans?"

"Yes."

"So why don't you think that we are morally obligated to go vegan?

Why doesn't, for example, our eating of animals represent the imposition of gratuitous suffering in the same way that torturing the dog does?"

"Because there's a huge difference with food because we need nutrition that we get from animals."

At this point, you discuss with the person how animal foods are not necessary for human nutrition. The discussion will always focus on some ground of supposed necessity and there's no purported ground that works. We explored just about every conceivable ground in *Eat Like You Care*. Frequently, you need to *patiently* engage and work through a series of these objections until you help the person see that what they thought were easy answers are no answers at all. If your discussion bounces through several of these points, stick with it! It means that you are speaking with someone who is willing to examine their own position and that can often lead to great results.

\*\*\*\*\*\*\*\*\*

In the next chapter, we will consider how to discuss the other Principles that make up the Abolitionist Approach.

# Chapter 12

## Some Thoughts on Advocating Other Aspects of the Abolitionist Approach

In this book, we have focused on veganism as a fundamental principle of justice, the right of animals not to be used as property, and the problems with the welfarist approach as a general matter. That covers the first three Principles of the Abolitionist Approach.

Here are some thoughts about, and on advocating concerning, the remaining three Principles. For a substantive discussion of these Principles—and all of the Six Principles—you should read our earlier book, *Animal Rights: The Abolitionist Approach*.

### Principle Four: Sentience

Principle Four: *The Abolitionist Approach links the moral status of nonhumans with sentience alone and not with any other cognitive characteristic; all sentient beings are equal for the purpose of not being used exclusively as a resource.*

Principle Four tells us that sentience is the *only* characteristic required to have the right not to be used exclusively as a resource.

Why is this Principle important?

It is important because there is a tendency to think that animals who are more "like us" matter more. Indeed, this is an idea that is promoted by many "animal advocates" who promote the idea that nonhuman great apes, dolphins and elephants matter more because they have more humanlike intelligence. Indeed, Peter Singer, so-called "father of the animal rights movement," maintains that killing animals is not harming them per se because animals are not self-aware in the way that humans are. He does, however, think that nonhuman great apes, elephants, and some marine mammals are self-aware and, at least with respect to nonhuman great apes, he seems to have a presumption against their use that comes close to (but is still not equivalent to) being like a right not to be used for human purposes.

Abolitionists reject this because they believe in the equality of *all* sentient beings for the purposes of not being used as a resource that has no value except its value to those who use it. This is not to say that Abolitionists believe that all animals are the same. They clearly are not. An elephant is different from a chicken. Elephants and chickens have different interests. An elephant does have more humanlike cognition than does a chicken. That, however, does not mean that the elephant matters more morally. For moral purposes of whether we can use the elephant or the chicken as a human resource, they are *completely* equal. Abolitionists maintain that we cannot treat *any* sentient being—irrespective of other cognitive or intellectual characteristics—as a thing or a resource. The fact that an animal is more "like us" is no more morally relevant for the use of that animal as a thing than is having lighter color skin and being more like white people relevant to whether someone should be a slave.

This exchange took place between Gary and a student at a lecture Gary was giving:

Student: "Do you agree with efforts to focus on nonhuman great apes for the purpose of establishing their personhood?"

Gary: "No, I don't."

"But you had a chapter in *The Great Ape Project* back in 1993."

"Yes, that's true. But even then, I expressed being uncomfortable with the idea that anything beyond sentience was necessary for full membership in the moral community. I expressed the view that sentience was sufficient."

"But don't you think there's a difference between a chimpanzee and a mouse?"

"Sure. There are lots of differences. They are two different species. They have different interests."

"But you don't think that the chimpanzee counts for more morally?"

"No, I don't, any more than I think that a human who is very intelligent counts for more morally than a person who is not intelligent or who may even be mentally disabled."

"But we treat humans differently. For example, we compensate someone who is a brain surgeon more than we do a janitor."

"That's true and that may be right or wrong depending on how you feel about the allocation of resources. But whatever you think on that point, we all agree that it is inappropriate to enslave a janitor to work for the brain surgeon or to kill the janitor to take his or her organs to save the life of the brain surgeon. For purposes of not being used exclusively as a resource, the brain surgeon and the janitor are equal."

"So you would not sacrifice an animal to save Einstein?"

"If what you are asking is whether I would regard, for example, killing a pig to remove a heart valve to save Einstein or any other person, as morally justifiable, the answer is no, I would not."

"That's extreme."

"You think so? Let me ask you, then, would you sacrifice someone you regarded as cognitively inferior to save Einstein? Would you take the heart valve out of a mentally disabled person to save Einstein?"

"No."

"Why not?"

"Because we shouldn't use any human that way."

"Precisely. That's exactly what I think, with the exception that I reject speciesism so I would apply that reasoning to nonhuman animals as well. I'm happy to believe that Einstein believed that too!"

## Principle Five: Human Rights and Animal Rights

Principle Five: *Abolitionists reject all forms of human discrimination, including racism, sexism, heterosexism, ageism, ableism, and classism—just as they reject speciesism.*

Principle Five says that Abolitionists reject all forms of human discrimination. The reason is simple. All forms of discrimination, including speciesism, function in the exact same way: they "otherize" someone or some group based on morally irrelevant criteria. That is, they designate some group as "other" based on these irrelevant criteria and then use that classification as a justification for treating the "other" as a resource or discounting their interests.

The Abolitionist Approach maintains that animal rights advocates must reject all commodification of any sentient being—human or nonhuman. Many "animal advocates" do not understand why Abolitionists are concerned about this issue.

Here is a discussion that Anna had with someone at a vegan event. This person had been a vegan for a number of years and fully agreed with the position that veganism is a moral imperative.

Vegan: "I am in agreement with your position on animal rights. But I can't agree with your view that we have some obligation to support feminism or to take a position on racism."

Anna: "Think about it this way. You object to speciesism, right?"

"Of course."

"Okay. And why do you object to speciesism?"

"Because species is irrelevant morally to the question of whether it is acceptable to treat a sentient being as a thing."

"So in this sense, speciesism is objectionable because it is like racism and sexism, which also involve the use of irrelevant criteria to justify treating other humans in an unacceptable way?"

"Yes."

"Well, then, don't you see where that leads? If speciesism is wrong because it is like racism and sexism, those of us who object to speciesism have already embraced a position on other forms of discrimination."

"Alright but does that mean that I need to be a campaigner for feminism and racial justice?"

"It means that you should be clear always in opposing sexism, racism, and other forms of discrimination. It does not mean that you have to stop being an advocate for animals and become active in other social justice movements, just as campaigners for other social justice movements do not have to stop their work to campaign for animals. As long as they stop eating, wearing, and using animals, and talk with others about their veganism, they can and should continue working on their human rights issues. As long as you do not use any form of discrimination in your advocacy, and as long as you make clear that, as an Abolitionist, you are opposed to all discrimination, no one is saying that you cannot be as a primary matter an advocate for animal rights and veganism."

## Principle Six: Violence

Principle Six: *Abolitionists recognize the principle of nonviolence as a core principle of the animal rights movement.*

Abolitionists are opposed to violence for three reasons.

*First,* in our view, the animal rights position is the ultimate rejection of violence. It is the ultimate affirmation of peace. We see the animal rights movement as the logical progression of the peace movement, which seeks to end conflict between humans. The animal rights movement ideally seeks to take that a step further and to end conflict between humans and nonhumans.

The reason why we are in the global mess that we are in now is that throughout history, we have engaged and continue to engage in violent actions that we have sought to justify as an undesirable means to a desirable end. Anyone who has ever used violence claims to regret having to resort to it, but argues that some desirable goal supposedly justified its use. The problem is that this facilitates an endless cycle of violence where anyone who feels strongly about something can embrace violence toward others as a means to achieving the greater good and those who are the targets of that violence may find a justification for their violent response. So on and on it goes.

Violence treats others as means to ends rather than as ends in themselves. When we engage in violence against others—whether they are human or nonhuman—we ignore their inherent value. We treat them only as *things* that have no value except that which we decide to give them. This is what leads people to engage in crimes of violence against people of color, women, and gay people and lesbians. It is what leads us to commodify nonhumans and treat them as resources that exist solely for our use. All of it is wrong and should be rejected.

*Second,* for those who advocate violence, exactly against whom is this violence to be directed? The farmer raises animals because the overwhelming number of humans demands to eat meat and animal products. The farmer raises those animals in intensive conditions because consumers want meat and animal products to be as inexpensive as possible. But is the farmer the only culprit here? Or is the responsibility shared by the rest of us who eat animal products, including all of those conscientious omnivores, the nonvegan "animal people" who consume "cage-free eggs" and "happy" meat, who create the demand but for which the farmer would be doing something else with their life? I suppose that it is easier to characterize farmers as the "enemy," but that ignores the reality of the situation.

What about the vivisector, a common target of those who advocate violence? Putting aside the debate about whether vivisection actually produces data useful to address problems of human health, most of the illnesses for which vivisectors are using animals are conditions that could be avoided entirely or drastically reduced if humans would stop eating animal foods, and engaging in such destructive behaviors as smoking, excessive alcohol consumption, drug use, and a failure to exercise. Again, who is the real culprit? We certainly do not think that vivisection is justifiable for any reason, but we find it curious that those who advocate violence can see vivisectors as detached from the social conditions that give rise to vivisection—and in these conditions we are all complicit.

*Third,* it is not clear to us what those who support violence hope to achieve as a practical matter. They certainly are not causing the public to become more sympathetic to the plight of nonhuman animals. If anything, the contrary is true and these actions have a most negative effect in terms of public perception. We live in a world where virtually anyone who can afford to eat animal products does so. There is no context in which violence can be interpreted in any way other than as negative.

In other words, when eating animal products is considered by most people as "natural" or "normal" as drinking water or breathing air, violence is quite likely to be seen as nothing more than an act of lunacy and will do nothing to further progressive thinking about the issue of animal exploitation. Animal exploitation is pervasive in our society. This is the case because we think that the ends (the supposed benefits we derive from animal use) justifies the means (imposing suffering and death on billions of nonhumans every year), and because we treat animals exclusively as commodities and ignore their inherent value. This situation cannot be meaningfully addressed by applying these notions to justify violence toward humans.

The fact that at least some "animal advocates" who endorse violence are not even vegan is truly bewildering. These people care so much about animals that they advocate inflicting harm on other humans who exploit nonhumans but cannot seem to stop exploiting nonhumans themselves.

The bottom line is clear. The only way that we are ever going to have a significant impact on the problem is through nonviolent education. That starts with our becoming vegans and rejecting violence against animals in our own lives, and spreads through creative, nonviolent vegan education.

In any event, if "animal advocates" embrace the idea that it's morally justifiable to use violence against "animal exploiters," then there is no principled way of deciding who is justly harmed and who is unjustly harmed.

Here is an example of a discussion that Gary had with someone who attended a lecture he gave several years ago at a Canadian university.

Supporter of violence: "If a vivisector is using sixty dogs a year in a horrible experiment, you don't think it's okay to kill or physically injure the vivisector, right?"

Gary: "Right. I think what the vivisector is doing is morally wrong but no, I don't think it's okay to use violence against the vivisector."

"Why not?"

"Let me ask you a question: are you a vegan?"

"Yes."

"Is your mother a vegan?"

"What does this have to do with my question?"

"It's directly related. I promise. Is she a vegan?"

"No, but she does not eat beef."

"Well, what animal products does your mom eat?"

"She eats chicken."

"Okay. Let's just focus on that for a second. Does she eat chicken several times a week?"

"Yes."

"Is it okay to use physical violence against your mother? She's responsible for many more deaths per year than is the vivisector in your question even if we focus only on her eating chicken and don't consider any other animal products."

"But that's different."

"How so? Your mother may be paying someone else to exploit the animal but, as a moral matter, she is just as responsible as the vivisector is."

"Well, it is different."

"I actually think that it is relevantly similar and I don't understand why you think it is different."

At this point, the person left the discussion so Gary never got an answer. But, to be frank, there is no good answer to his question. The only coherent answer is to say that it is morally acceptable to use violence against anyone who is not a vegan. And that answer, although coherent, raises other issues.

In any event, the Abolitionist Approach maintains that violence is the problem, and not the solution, and that violence against "animal exploiters," which means anyone who is not vegan, is not going to be an answer to the problem of violence against nonhumans.

# Conclusion

In this book, we have provided you with the basic tools that you need to go out and advocate for Abolitionist veganism. We have two final comments.

*First,* we want to return to an idea that we raised in the Introduction: if we are ever going to change the world and stop the exploitation of animals, *each one of us* has to participate. It's not a matter of writing a check to some bloated corporate charity. It's a matter of a grassroots movement building and establishing veganism as a moral imperative that is recognized by everyone who cares about animals and who believes that they have moral value.

*The effort begins with you.*

*Second,* we want to address a question that we get all the time. People ask us, "How is it that you haven't burned out over these past 35 years? Don't you find doing animal work really stressful and depressing?"

This is a complicated and difficult question but it is an important one. The answer is, yes, of course, we find it stressful and depressing in the way that focusing on any injustice that can't be stopped immediately is an occasion of prolonged sadness. Trying to address the problem in a world in which most people think that it is fine to exploit animals is stressful.

But we have always considered it an honor to do what we do in the service of animals.

And we have never seen "burning out" as an option.

We are not the ones waiting in a holding pen who will be slaughtered tomorrow morning.

We are not the ones being confined on a factory farm or some supposedly more "humane" alternative.

We are not the cow whose calf is taken away hours after birth; we are not the calf who is separated from her or his mother and who is terrified.

We are not the debeaked chickens confined in some battery cage or in an "enriched" cage or in one large cage called a "cage-free" barn.

We are not the animals being exploited in laboratories.

We are not the sheep being exploited for their wool, or the animals exploited for their leather or fur.

We are not the animals being exploited in circuses, zoos, animal fighting businesses, rodeos, aquaria, etc.

We are not the animals being hunted.

We have no right to burn out.

We cannot burn out.

We have an obligation to get up every single morning and start it all again and go out there in an effort to see that justice is done and the victimization of the vulnerable ends.

We see every person we meet as someone who has the ability to share the vision we have. We see every person as someone who can care about morality and can transform her or his life as a result of that caring.

We see every person as having a spark that we must ignite.

And we have no choice but to try.

For the billions at risk at this very moment, and for the unimaginable numbers of animals in the future, we cannot ever see failure—or our inaction—as an option.

*Now, please, for the sake of all the animals who are exploited every second of every minute of every hour of every day: get out there and advocate.*

*The World is Vegan! If **you** want it.*

# Appendix 1

## The Six Principles of the Abolitionist Approach

**Principle One:** *Abolitionists maintain that all sentient beings, human or nonhuman, have one right—the basic right not to be treated as the property of others.*

Animals are classified as property and are used exclusively as resources for humans. Although we claim to regard animals as having moral value and to not be just things, their status as property means that they have no moral value; they have only economic value. We recognize that treating humans as property is inconsistent with recognizing humans as members of the moral community. We accept as a fundamental moral principle that all humans, irrespective of their particular characteristics, must be accorded the basic moral right not to be property. On this principle rests the universal condemnation of human slavery. The property status of animals means that animals are considered to be things, irrespective of what we say to the contrary. There is no way to distinguish humans from nonhumans that can justify withholding from all sentient nonhumans the same right that we accord to all humans. We need to recognize that all sentient beings are equal for the purpose of not being used exclusively as human resources. The Abolitionist Approach maintains that all animal use—however supposedly "humane"—is morally unjustified.

**Principle Two:** *Abolitionists maintain that our recognition of this one basic right means that we must abolish, and not merely regulate, institution-alized animal exploitation, and that Abolitionists should not support welfare reform campaigns or single-issue campaigns.*

Recognizing the right of animals not to be used as property requires that we *abolish* the institutionalized exploitation of nonhuman animals, and not just regulate it to make it more "humane." Abolitionists reject animal welfare campaigns. They also reject single-issue campaigns, a particular sort of regulatory campaign that characterizes certain forms of animal exploitation as different from, and worse than, other forms of exploitation and which suggests, by implication, that other forms of exploitation are acceptable. Both welfare campaigns and single-issue campaigns actually *promote* animal exploitation and result in partnerships between supposed animal advocates and institutionalized exploiters.

**Principle Three:** *Abolitionists maintain that veganism is a moral baseline and that creative, nonviolent vegan education must be the cornerstone of rational animal rights advocacy.*

Abolitionists embrace the idea that there is veganism and there is animal exploitation: there is no third choice. To not be a vegan is to participate directly in animal exploitation. Abolitionists promote veganism as a moral baseline or a moral imperative and as the *only* rational response to the recognition that animals have moral value. If animals matter morally, then we cannot treat them as commodities and eat, wear, or use them. Just as someone who promoted the abolition of slavery could not own slaves, an Abolitionist with respect to animal slavery cannot consume animal products. For an Abolitionist, veganism is a fundamental matter of justice. As the Abolitionist Approach is a grassroots movement, advocating veganism as a fundamental principle of justice is not something that requires large, wealthy charities and "leaders." It is something that we all can do and must do as a grassroots movement. Each of us must be a leader.

**Principle Four:** *The Abolitionist Approach links the moral status of nonhumans with sentience alone and not with any other cognitive characteris-tic; all sentient beings are equal for the purpose of not being used exclusively* *as a resource.*

Sentience is subjective awareness; there is some*one* who perceives and experiences the world. A sentient being has interests; that is, preferences, wants, or desires. If a being is sentient, then that is necessary and sufficient for the being to have the right not to be used as a means to human ends. The recognition of this right imposes on humans the moral obligation not to use that being as a resource. It is not necessary for a sentient being to have humanlike cognitive characteristics in order to be accorded the right not to be used as property.

**Principle Five:** *Abolitionists reject all forms of human discrimination, including racism, sexism, heterosexism, ageism, ableism, and classism—just as they reject speciesism.*

The Abolitionist Approach to Animal Rights rejects speciesism because, like racism, sexism, heterosexism, and other forms of human discrimination, it uses a morally irrelevant criterion (species) to discount and devalue the interests of sentient beings. But any opposition to speciesism makes sense *only* as part of a general opposition to all forms of discrimination. That is, we *cannot* oppose speciesism but claim that, as animal advocates, we do not have a position on these other forms of discrimination. We cannot say that we regard species as a morally objectionable criterion used to discount or devalue the interests of nonhumans but that we do not have a position on whether race, sex, or sexual orientation/preference are morally objectionable criteria when used to discount or devalue human interests. Our opposition to speciesism *requires* that we oppose *all* discrimination.

**Principle Six:** *Abolitionists recognize the principle of nonviolence as a core principle of the animal rights movement.*

The Abolitionist Approach promotes nonviolence because it sees the animal rights movement as an extension of the peace movement to include concerns about nonhuman animals. Moreover, given that most people engage in animal exploitation, there is no principled way to distinguish exploiters for the purpose of justifying violence. Finally, because there is pervasive exploitation, violence cannot be understood as anything but a pathological reaction to what is regarded as normal. The only real option is, on the individual level, to embrace veganism as a moral baseline and, on the social level, to engage in creative, nonviolent vegan education from an Abolitionist perspective.

# Appendix 2

## Ten Logical Fallacies

There is a great deal that one could say about the topic of logical reasoning, including the observation that we don't seem to see a great deal of it in modern discourse! Indeed, one could teach an entire course in logic based on the logical errors found in a single news broadcast, a politician's speech, or the editorial page of just about any major newspaper. Many of the arguments that you will encounter when you do Abolitionist vegan advocacy exhibit logical problems of various sorts. Understanding logic is very important for effective advocacy on any topic, including Abolitionist vegan advocacy.

In this appendix, we will consider a very small part of the topic: we will review ten of what are called "informal fallacies." These are fallacies that involve defects in reasoning that can be detected only by examining the content of an argument and are not merely a matter of a defective argument structure. If you understand how to address these fallacies, you will be a much more effective advocate.

# 1. Appeal to Pity

The Appeal to Pity fallacy occurs when someone tries to use pity from a listener to support agreement with a conclusion.

*Example 1:* "I am not guilty of violating animal rights by not being vegan because I really love animals and I have several rescued dogs and cats. I take very good care of these animals and last year alone, I spent over $10,000 for their veterinary care and that required great sacrifice on my part and I had to forego medical care for myself to provide for them."

We have all heard some version of this many times. The conclusion—that the person is not violating animal rights by not being vegan—is not supported logically by the claims, even if true, about the speaker's circumstances. Whether the speaker makes sacrifices for their dogs is logically irrelevant to whether the person is violating animal rights by not being vegan. This fallacy involves a psychological appeal in that if the listener feels pity for the speaker, they will be more likely to accept the conclusion.

*Example 2:* "It's okay that I am not vegan because, if I were to go vegan, my family would disown me and I really love my family and would be lost without their support."

The conclusion that it is morally acceptable to not be vegan does not follow logically from the claims about family reaction. The speaker is trying to get the listener to accept the conclusion as a result of pitying the speaker's situation.

# 2. Appeal to Popularity

There are different versions of this fallacy but the one we want to focus on involves what is called the "bandwagon argument," which involves the speaker arguing that the listener ought to come to some conclusion because everybody else has come to that conclusion.

*Example 1:* "Your position on veganism is just wrong. Almost everyone eats, wears, and uses animal products."

So what? Most people embrace some form of sexism. Should we reject equality because lots of other people do? Many people are still racist. Does that mean that we should embrace racism because lots of other people do?

The fact that "everybody" believes something does not make it right.

*Example 2:* "Abolitionist vegans reject welfare reform campaigns and single-issue campaigns. But all of the large animal charities support these campaigns and, therefore, Abolitionist vegans must be wrong."

Again, the fact that all of the large animal charities embrace welfare reform campaigns and single-issue campaigns is not logical support for the position that animal advocates should support those campaigns. A central argument of the Abolitionist Approach is that these corporate charities promote those sorts of campaigns to maximize fundraising campaigns precisely because they make people feel more comfortable about continuing to exploit animals.

Another version of this fallacy is the "tradition argument," where someone tries to justify some practice on the ground that it has been done as a matter of tradition.

*Example 1:* "There is nothing wrong with killing and eating animals. We've been doing that for thousands of years."

The fact that something has been going on for a long time does not mean that it is a morally good thing. Sexism and racism have been around in various forms for a long time as well.

*Example 2:* "Serving turkey on Thanksgiving is traditional. Therefore, it is perfectly fine as a moral matter."

Again, the fact that eating a turkey on Thanksgiving is a tradition says nothing about whether we should continue to exploit animals on Thanksgiving (or at any other time).

A third version of this fallacy is the "culture argument," where someone argues that some practice is acceptable because it is part of a culture.

*Example:* "Veganism is not a moral imperative because eating meat and other animal foods is an important part of my culture."

Female genital mutilation is an accepted cultural practice in some places. Does that make it right?

## 3. Argument Against the Person

There are several types of this argument as well. All forms share the characteristic that the person making the argument directs the listener away from the substantive point and toward the personal characteristic of someone who advances the substantive point. The idea is to persuade the listener to reject a position not based on its merits, but on some supposed personal defect on the part of person promoting the position.

*Example 1:* "I was thinking about going vegan but I can't stand vegans because they yell at people."

These days, many people equate anyone disagreeing with them as "yelling." But, putting that aside, there is no doubt that some vegans do engage in uncivil forms of discourse, which is rejected by the Abolitionist Approach. However, even if some vegans are rude and offensive, that has absolutely nothing to do logically with the validity of their position.

*Example 2:* "The Abolitionist argument that veganism is a moral imperative is wrong because Abolitionists are just 'purists.'"

If the Abolitionist argument on this (or any) point is invalid, an argument must be offered. It does not suffice to say call Abolitionists a name.

*Example 3:* "You Abolitionists reject the position of the corporate charities because Abolitionism is a cult and you are just trying to get people to accept only your view and not to explore others."

The arguer is claiming that the Abolitionist position on the large corporate charities is wrong because Abolitionism is a "cult." That does not address the arguments that Abolitionists make against these charities and asks the listener to conclude that Abolitionists are wrong because they are "bad" people—they are involved in a "cult."

In addition to being fallacious, this argument is ironic in that a hallmark of cults is the rejection of reasoning. The large corporate charities will not tolerate any questioning of their approach. To question is to be "divisive" and to be acting to "harm" animals. One must just accept unquestioningly. The Abolitionist position welcomes reasoned discussion. If someone disagrees with the Abolitionist position on corporate charities, they need to present an argument against that position and not just express some verbal abuse against Abolitionists.

*Example 4:* "Abolitionists say that we should try to eat healthy foods but I know Abolitionists who eat lots of vegan junk foods."

Abolition is about nonviolence: to others; to self; to the planet that sustains all sentient life. Abolitionists maintain that we should be concerned primarily about violence to sentient others, but they also maintain that we should not engage in violence against ourselves. The fact that some Abolitionists may eat a lot of junk food does not invalidate that point.

## 4. Straw Man

This fallacy involves distorting an opponent's argument to make it easier to attack.

*Example 1:* "We should reject the Abolitionist position that veganism is a moral imperative because not everyone will go vegan overnight."

No one maintains that everyone—or even many people—will go vegan "overnight." This argument attempts to get people to reject the Abolitionist Approach because it supposedly requires that we believe that people will go vegan "overnight." Some people will go vegan immediately; many won't. That's not the point. The Abolitionist Approach maintains that we ought to be clear that, if people agree that animals matter morally, they are morally obligated to go vegan. This is no different from saying that we ought to promote equality as a moral imperative even if many people will continue to be racist or sexist. But in none of these cases is anyone claiming that promoting the moral imperative depends on whether everyone will vegan (or stop being racist or sexist) overnight.

*Example 2:* "We should reject the Abolitionist Approach because Abolitionists oppose domestication and we cannot just let all domesticated animals wander around."

The Abolitionist position is that domestication cannot be morally justified. See https://goo.gl/4oTC6c. But that does not mean that we should free all domesticated animals. We should care for the animals who are presently in existence but we should not facilitate the production of more domesticated animals. We cannot let all domesticated animals roam freely. They are domesticated animals and have been bred to be dependent on us.

## 5. Red Herring

This fallacy involves the person making the argument completely changing the original subject and hoping that the listener does not see the change.

*Example:* "Abolitionists claim that veganism is a moral imperative. But if we look at the present political scene, we see that fundamentalism is on the rise and is resulting in terrorism. We need to reject fundamentalism."

The original point concerns the Abolitionist claim that veganism is a moral imperative. The person making the argument then changes the subject and starts talking about fundamentalism, drawing a conclusion about that subject that has nothing to do with the assertion of a moral principle. In order to eliminate the fallacy, the arguer would have to maintain that the assertion of this moral principle is relevantly analogous to religious fundamentalism. The arguer wants to avoid that because it is a silly position to take. So the arguer uses the Red Herring fallacy.

## 6. Appeal to Unqualified Authority

This fallacy involves trying to get someone to accept a conclusion based on an authority that lacks credibility because of a lack of expertise, a lack of competence, clear bias, or clear motivation to lie and, therefore, is not credible.

*Example 1:* Nicolette, who raises animals for slaughter, says that it's perfectly fine to eat animals and, indeed, the animals don't mind being killed and eaten. Therefore, we should believe her and conclude that animals don't mind being killed and eaten.

Nicolette is clearly biased and her statements cannot be trusted. Moreover, she has an incentive to lie in this situation.

*Example 2:* Bill, who runs an intensive chicken operation with hundreds of thousands of birds, says that his operation has no negative environmental consequences. Therefore, we should conclude that Bill's chicken ranch does not have negative environmental consequences.

Bill has an incentive to lie in this situation. He may be correct as to the lack of negative consequences (although he is not!). But that would require an independent investigation. We cannot appeal to Bill's position alone to show this is the case.

## 7. Hasty Generalization

This fallacy occurs when the sample that is offered to justify the conclusion is not representative of the group.

*Example:* "Veganism is unhealthy. I knew someone who was a vegan who had terrible health."

Putting aside that we don't know what sort of vegan this person was (that is, did the person only eat iceberg lettuce and water?), we cannot draw any conclusion from a sample of one.

## 8. Slippery Slope

This fallacy is committed when the conclusion of an argument rests on there being a chain reaction where there is insufficient reason to believe that the chain reaction will, in fact, take place.

*Example 1:* "We must reject the Abolitionist Approach position because, if we agree that animals have the fundamental right not to be used as resources, that will lead to humans being devalued."

We often hear this sort of argument from people who are religious. They claim that recognizing the moral value of nonhumans will lead to the devaluation of humans. There is, however, no reason to believe such a claim.

*Example 2:* "We must reject the Abolitionist Approach because, if we agree that animals have the fundamental right not to be used as resources, that will result in animals getting all sorts of rights and this will lead to social chaos and will be unworkable."

Again, there is simply no reason to believe that recognizing the fundamental right not to be used as property will lead to giving nonhuman animals the right to vote or drive cars.

## 9. Begging the Question

This fallacy, like many others, has a number of forms. One that is encountered frequently in the animal context involves when the conclusion of an argument merely restates a false or questionable premise—the argument effectively assumes the truth of the conclusion.

*Example:* "It is morally acceptable to exploit animals because they are inferior to humans."

This argument has the conclusion that it is morally acceptable to exploit animals. And what's the support for that? The support is the premise that animals are inferior to us. So the conclusion is just restating the premise that supposedly supports it.

## 10. False Dichotomy

This fallacy involves presenting two unlikely alternatives as the only ones available and then choosing the one that the arguer prefers.

*Example:* "Either we campaign for the 'humane' treatment of animals or animals will suffer horribly. We don't want animals to suffer horribly so we must campaign for the 'humane' treatment of animals."

This is problematic in two respects. First, it assumes that we can stop horrible suffering by campaigning for the "humane" treatment of animals. If animals continue to be used as human resources, they will continue to suffer horribly irrespective of how "humane" our treatment is.

Second, it ignores that the choice is not limited in the way that is presented. There is another—and much better option—we campaign for veganism and persuade people not to eat, wear, or use animals.

# Other Resources

**Books:**

*Animal Rights: The Abolitionist Approach (2015)*
www.abolitionistapproachbook.com
*Eat Like You Care: An Examination of the Morality of Eating Animals (2013)*
www.eatlikeyoucarebook.com

**Websites:**

www.abolitionistapproach.com
www.howdoigovegan.com

**Other websites (in English) that promote an Abolitionist position:**

www.ecorazzi.com
www.internationalvegan.org

**Facebook:**

www.facebook.com/abolitionistapproach
www.facebook.com/howdoigovegan
www.facebook.com/eatlikeyoucare
www.facebook.com/abolitionistapproachbook
www.facebook.com/abolitionistapproachtranslated
www.facebook.com/advocateforanimalsBook

**Twitter:**

www.twitter.com/garylfrancione
www.twitter.com/howdoigovegan

**Instagram:**

www.instagram.com/gary.francione

www.instagram.com/howdoigovegandotcom

www.instagram.com/abolitionistapproachtranslated

**Video:**

**Introductory videos**

*Introduction to the Abolitionist Approach to Animal Rights:*
www.youtube.com/watch?v=Ym-jWBYQxeI
*The Abolitionist Approach to Animal Rights and Veganism as a Moral Imperative:* www.youtube.com/watch?v=NN7xfVJom98
*The Animal Rights "Movement": Moving Backwards:*
www.youtube.com/watch?v=Q9M0Ms3YLaE

**Official video sites**

www.vimeo.com/garylfrancione

www.youtube.com/garylfrancionevegan

Many videos also available at www.abolitionistapproach.com

**Podcasts:**

www.blubrry.com/abolitionistapproachcommentary

http://itunes.apple.com/WebObjects/MZStore.woa/wa/viewPod-cast?id=327041563

Podcasts are also available at www.abolitionistapproach.com

**Vegan Recipes:**

www.howdoigovegan.com/vegan-recipes/

**QR Codes:**

Abolitionist
Approach

HowDoIGoVegan

Vegan Recipes

The Abolitionist
Approach to Animal
Rights and Veganism
as a Moral Imperative

The Animal Rights
"Movement":
Moving Backwards

Introduction to
the Abolitionist
Approach to
Animal Rights

# About the Authors

Gary L. Francione is Board of Governors Distinguished Professor of Law and the Nicholas deB. Katzenbach Scholar of Law and Philosophy at Rutgers University School of Law. He is also Honorary Professor (Philosophy) at the University of East Anglia in Norwich, Norfolk, UK.

Anna Charlton is an attorney and Adjunct Professor of Law at Rutgers University School of Law. She was the co-founder and co-director (with Gary L. Francione) of the Rutgers Animal Rights Law Clinic.

abolitionistapproach.com
howdoIgovegan.com
international vegan.org
voxvegan.com

—

Gary Steiner @ Bucknell
for scholarship

Made in the USA
Columbia, SC
27 January 2019